Re-bek'ah

The Resurrection of Jesus Christ

by Darrell Gilbert

TATE PUBLISHING, LLC

Introduction

The purpose of this book is to introduce to the reader the covenant of God with Abraham, the faith of Jesus Christ. Most of what is written in this book were originally e-mails sent to members of a bible study class. My hope is that this will give the beginning Christian a good foundation for understanding the scriptures, and challenge the beliefs of those who already have a basic understanding of scriptures. Some of these letters were written to very prominent and highly respected teachers. It is strongly suggested that if you don't understand something to move on. Concentrating on it too hard may lead to confusion or stress. Come back to it, as very likely it will be explained later. The reader should make a commitment right now to themselves not to quit reading this book until they at least read it twice. This is an entirely new and different way of understanding the death and resurrection of Jesus Christ. Any person who already knows everything, or is not open to the possibility that the scriptures can say more than just one thing, will likely reject everything written here. I wish to say now that I fully believe with all my heart that Jesus Christ died and rose again for me, and that I am saved by this. It is imperative that you <u>make</u> time, at least one hour every day, to sit alone somewhere with no disturbances whatsoever. All problems of the day or possible problems should be discarded. If you do not commit to doing these things daily, the book will have less of an impact. At times this doctrine is very blunt and may be quite offensive or unpopular. I try to give scripture to back up every little thing I say. Not just a scripture out of the blue, but this is a verse by verse interpretation of primarily the entire book of Galatians. I also compare the scriptures found in Galatians with similar scriptures out of other books from both the old and new testaments to give a more complete and accurate interpretation, and to give assurance of that accuracy. Please, please have a King James Bible open and read the verses in and around what is discussed, even if you insist on having another translation by it. Because of the ancient language of this version it is sometimes hard to understand, but due to the unsurpassed accuracy from a word for word translation I chose this version. It was not translated by reading a part and giving an opinion on what it might say, but word for word, with less regard to whether the translator understood it. Some of these words are very large but have great meaning to them. I feel that once a reader gets used to the version, and understands just a few basic word adjustments, the King James is well worth the trouble. There is a little King James Help included. Also, I have defined the words that are large and complicated. Although I have included a mini dictionary at the end, it is also strongly suggested that you have a dictionary on hand.

King James Help

Just these few simple things are all that you need to know, and you should easily understand this very accurate version.

-Do not pay too much attention to the way the scripture is punctuated.

-Words put in italics are to let the reader know that they were added to the original word for word translation, they were not a part of the original text.

-When *th, eth,* or the letter *t,* is located at the end of a word (such as in becometh, hast, or shalt) just drop it or replace with *s.*

<u>afore</u>: before; previously

<u>behold</u>: "check this out," or "look!" Often used term when wanting you to pay close attention to the phrase following.

<u>even</u>: a word sometimes used between phrases to emphasize what follows. For example: he looked content, <u>even</u> happy. Or: Christ is ***a stone of stumbling, <u>even</u> to them which stumble at the word, being disobedient: whereunto they were also appointed. (1 Peter 2:8)***

<u>for</u>: because

<u>furthermore</u> or <u>moreover</u>: a word telling you that what is about to be said is a further comment hav-

ing to do with what was just stated. More added over and above what was said.

<u>henceforth</u>: from here on out; from this point forward.

<u>hereunto</u>: to here

<u>mine</u>: my

<u>shall, shalt</u>: will; should

<u>therefore, wherefore</u>: for this reason; so then

<u>thou, thee, thine, thy, thyself</u>: you, yours, your, yourself.

<u>unto</u>: to

<u>whereunto</u>: unto where

<u>whosoever</u>: whoever

<u>ye</u>: you

The rest, if any, you should easily figure out.

Prayers

I pray that you would take me, this sin that's in me, and crucify me on the cross with you, that we would die together on the cross. That we would be buried, and that you would lift only you up from death in me, and me in you. Please live my life in me for me which I now give to you, that I might live only for you.

I pray that you would wash my mind with your blood, and cleanse my heart with your pure water. Put my trust in you for me. Grant me your Spirit, and manifest your Spirit in me that I might know and understand the truth, and so I might believe the truth. I pray that I might have only truth and that you would show me where I am wrong.

Tell me your will for me, also for the world. Let me see life, others, me, and you like you do. Let me understand you Lord . . . the way that you are, the things that you do, have done, and are going to do and why. Remind me of all the things that you've taught me and how. Grant me assurance of all things and keep me from confusion and doubt.

By your truth Lord, grant me humility in heart and mind. Show me your mercy and your love. Cause me to feel love for you . . . pure, real, powerful love and increase it more and more along with all your fruits. Let me be patient, toward life, you, and myself. And so that I may forgive others. Fill me with grateful-ness and hope, sincerity, and peace of mind.

Give me understanding of your way of faith, show me how to apply it in life, guide me by them. Show me when I am about to sin before I sin. Let me be complete and constant in your ways. Commit me totally and only to you Lord, give me a heart to be faithful to you. To seek after you with all my heart and to wait for you daily in reading, praying, think-ing, and keeping your commandments. Cause me to think about you constantly. To be open to not just being righteous, but holy. Show me that I am on the right path.

Strengthen me Lord to do your will. Show me the difference between my will and yours. Let me not lie to myself. Teach me Lord. Open my eyes to your words. Astonish me with your wisdom. Show me awesome things. Whisper them in my ear that I may rejoice in you intensely and praise you for your gen-tleness, your kindness, your mercy, and love. Show me what I don't see.

Reveal your power to me Lord, your awesome power. Let me experience it that I may respect you and fear you. Show me that you are there, and that you are watching me, and don't hide your face from me. Talk to me Lord, let me hear your voice for real.

Lord, please give me a gift, something spiritual that I may give to others, that you may give me more. Use me for good, prepare me so that I may be profit-able to your body and bring honor to you. Protect me. Grant me courage and willingness to overcome sufferings and every situation. And let me know that you have answered me. In Jesus' name.

1 Corinthians 5:6 know ye not that a little leaven leaveneth the whole lump? I know that you know Paul is using an Old Testament scripture to explain a spiritual truth. A little leaven, (wickedness), makes the whole lump, (the body of Christ), corrupt. That leaven comes from one member, a person. *5:7 Purge out therefore the old leaven, that ye may be a new lump, as ye are unleavened. For even Christ our Passover is sacrificed for us.* As you also know, in the Old Testament law it was commanded in *Exodus 12* for the Jews to keep the feast of the Passover. Before the feast they ate leavened bread, then they slaughtered a lamb, then could not eat but only unleavened bread for seven days afterward. This was all a physical example of things spiritual that were to come, a literal law that we are to keep <u>forever</u> spiritually as commanded in *Exodus 12:14 ye shall keep it a feast by an ordinance forever.* That lamb represented the spiritual and true lamb, Christ, as it says: *Christ, our Passover, is sacrificed for us.* So from here on out, we who are God's chosen, the spiritual Jew, (Christians), who have eaten, (received within us spiritually), our Passover lamb, (Christ), are not allowed to eat leavened bread, (or accept within our bodies any wickedness), till the seventh day, the time of Christ's return. We who have Christ's blood smeared on the doorposts, (our heart), of our house, (which is what we dwell in, our physical body), are to keep that law of the feast <u>forever</u> in Spirit and Truth. And as God said in *Exodus 12:15 For whosoever eateth leavened bread from the first day until the seventh day shall be cut off from Israel.* Then we should cut off those Christians, as Paul did in *1 Cor. 5:3–5,* who eat leavened bread during this week, and have no part with them. We should not fellowship or keep company with them . . ."eat" with them. *1 Cor. 5:8: therefore let us keep the feast, not with old leaven, neither with the leaven of malice and wickedness, but with the unleavened bread of sincerity and truth. 5:11 Now I have written to you not to keep company with* that wicked *brother, with such a one no, not to eat.* Furthermore, prophecy: *Exodus 12:16 And in the first day there shall be a holy convocation.* This was done the first day, in the time of Jesus and the Apostles as *Exodus 12:15* says: *the first day ye shall put away leaven out of your houses. Ex. 12:16 And in the seventh day there shall be a holy convocation.* And so similarly that leavened bread, that Wicked will be cast out shortly as Satan was then. You have admitted the condition of the church, but I think the time of the latter rain is near. *James 5:7*

==

Exodus 12:16 And in the seventh day there shall be a holy convocation. As when Christ came, now, and when Christ comes. The book of Hebrews talks a lot of what will happen on the last day. *Hebrews 4:4 For He spake in a certain place of the seventh day in this way: And God did rest the seventh day from all his works.* As explained before, the things that happened in the Old Testament tell in a literal way what will happen spiritually. It serves as an <u>example</u> of things to come. What God did on the seventh day is what his people do at the last time: *Heb. 4:10 For he that is entered into His rest,* meaning heaven, *he also has ceased from his own works, <u>as God did from His.</u>* This is also saying that those who have made it to an eternal rest have also stopped doing their own works of evil. They also have <u>rested</u> from their works. *4:3 For we which have believed do enter into rest,* we quit doing evil. *Heb. 3:7 Therefore, (as the Holy Ghost says, <u>Today,</u> if you will hear His voice, harden not your hearts, as in the provocation, in the day of temptation in the wilderness when your fathers tested me. So I was grieved, and swore in wrath that they shall not enter into my rest.)* This event occurred in the book of *Numbers 14* The children of Israel disobeyed God's commandment and provoked God. It is commonly known that the land of Egypt was a representation of death. Pharaoh represented Satan. Moses was the example of Christ. The land of Canaan is the literal example of the true and spiritual promised land: heaven. The Jews were the example of Christians. Just as God delivered the Jews and baptized them in the Red Sea into the wilderness, He also has done spiritually to us through Christ. And in the same way we have not yet been fully delivered, though we have. We are in the wilderness because we are not dead fully; we have not

Re-bek'ah

13

entered heaven. God through Moses preached the gospel to the Jews, promising them that he would give them a land flowing with milk and honey. Only when it came time and God commanded them to enter and possess it, they were disobedient to God and rebelled. They rebelled because they feared, saying that God was not able to give them the land and defeat the people who were there already. In their disobedience they were saying that they didn't believe in God. *Numbers 14:11 And the Lord said unto Moses, How long will this people provoke me? And how long will it be until they believe me? 14:12 I will smite them, and disinherit them. 14:22 Because all those which have seen my glory and miracles which I did in Egypt and the wilderness, and have tempted me now these ten times, 14:23 surely they shall not see the land which I sware unto their fathers, none that provoked me.* So here it explains that though God had sworn to them, and though they were His people, because they provoked God through their disobedience and unbelief He denied them access to His promise. *Numbers 14:29 Your carcases shall fall in this wilderness, 14:30 doubtless ye shall not come into the land which I sware to make you dwell therein. 14:34 And ye shall know my breach of promise.* Their disobedience to God's commands of faith showed that they did not believe in God. In the same way, God has spoken to us that same gospel, only not the example but the true and real faith: *Hebrews 4:2 For unto us was the gospel preached, as well as unto them.* So in the same way, when we obey Christ, we say by our actions that we really believe what was told to us about Him, that He can give us the promise of the Father, the Spirit. And when we believe in Jesus, we say that God's word is true, that He spoke what would happen in the scriptures, and that He raised Him from the dead; we believe in God. So says *Hebrews 3:12 Take heed, brethren, lest there be in any of you an evil heart of unbelief in departing from the living God.* So in departing from God, in disobedience to God, there is unbelief. *4:11: Let us <u>labour</u> therefore to enter into that rest, unless anyone fall after the same <u>example</u> of unbelief,* unless we also deny the truth as the children of Israel. *Hebrews 3:13 But exhort one another daily, while it is called <u>today,</u> lest any of you be hardened through the deceitfulness of sin. 3:14 For we are made partakers of Christ if we hold the beginning of our confidence steadfast to the end.*

===========

Hebrews 3:15 Today, if ye will hear His voice, harden not your hearts, as in the provocation. 3:16 Some, when they heard, provoked, but not all that came out of Egypt by Moses. 3:17–19 But to whom was He grieved? Was it not to them that <u>sinned</u>? Whose carcasses fell in the wilderness? And to whom sware He that they should not enter into rest but to them that <u>believed not</u>? "Sin" and "believe not" go hand in hand. And these are His people, being delivered from bondage out of Egypt and from Pharaoh. *Heb. 4:1 Let us therefore fear, lest, a promise being left of entering into rest, any of you should seem to come short of it. For the word preached did not profit them, not being mixed with faith, 4:3 For we which have believed do enter into rest,* we cease from our old works. Folks, there is a healthy fear, and there is a fear that is not healthy. And as God did rest from His works from the foundation of the world, even so those who are God's rest from the foundation of the world. Before they were born, it was ordained that we would rest, *4:3 the works were finished from the foundation of the world. 4:6 Seeing therefore it remains that some must enter therein.* This is saying that because God ceased from His works, and this is a pattern of things to come spiritually, and the scripture cannot be broken, then there must be a period of time, a <u>day</u> that a people would stop doing wickedly and enter into rest, the last day. *4:6 and they to whom it was first preached entered not in because of unbelief.* So the writer of Hebrews gets here that there is still an opening, a day that would be holy. He gets that the time of Moses and those people was not that day because they did not rest: *4:8–9 For if Jesus had given them rest, he would not have afterward spoken of another day.* When did he speak of another day? *Hebrews 4:7* quotes a Psalm, which was written after the events and time of Moses: *Today, after so long a time, Today, if ye will hear His voice, harden not your hearts.* So he is saying that the seventh day has not come in his time and that there was still a chance to make it to heaven: *4:9 there remains therefore a rest to the people of God.* So I say that it could very well be that these very things have happened again, and that the writer lived in the first day, as I wrote in the last e-mail: *the first day is when evil shall be put away from your houses.* Then I say also that according to the pattern there remains still to this day a rest to us, because Jesus spoke of another day during His generation. And again, *4:6 They to whom it was first preached entered not in because of unbelief.*

How was the gospel preached to that generation? Using examples as shown above. The scriptures foretold of what would happen and did during the generation of Jesus. But these things were hidden to the natural, or carnal mind, from those who only saw in the literal or physical sense. They were revealed to those whom God chose to show them to through the Spirit. The things that happened in the past and are recorded in the bible are a pattern of what is to come spiritually. They aren't the actual thing, but a shadow of the real. And indeed the faith people had during that day justified them before God until the real came into being, because in the day that faith was, it was real. The covenant that God justified His people under was the covenant established with a man named Abraham. Paul the Apostle in the New Testament explained this faith that Abraham had which was written in the Old Testament: *Romans 4:19 And being not weak in faith, he considered not*

his own body now dead, when he was about an hundred years old, neither yet the deadness of Sarah's womb, 4:20 He staggered not at the promise of God through unbelief. This happened in ***Genesis 17.*** God had promised Abraham when he was younger that He would give him a child, or a <u>seed</u>, that He would give the land of Israel too, which is called the promised land. But it didn't come to pass, to the point that now it was deemed too late because Abraham grew too old to have children. His body and his wife Sarah's womb were now <u>dead</u>. Yet God said that He would still do it, so He gave a command for Abraham to do which was according to His word, that Abraham should circumcise all that were his. And so even though Abraham originally doubted and laughed at that gospel told to him by God (that He could raise his body from its dead state), he circumcised himself and all that were in his house as God commanded. Because Abraham kept the law of circumcision, he said by his actions that he believed God. And because he believed, God said he was just before Him: ***Romans 4:21 And being fully persuaded that what He had promised He was able also to perform, 4:22: therefore it was counted to him for righteousness.*** Again the faith that would give life was foretold when Abraham offered his only begotten son as a sacrifice ***(Hebrews 11:17–19).*** After God had given Abraham a son, Isaac, He commanded Abraham to kill him. If Isaac were dead then the only way God could give Isaac the promised land was to raise him from the dead. But Abraham believed God could raise his son from the dead, and so he obeyed God's commandment of faith. And because Abraham believed, God swore with an oath that to him and his seed He would give the promised land . . . life. So the covenant of faith was established, that all who believed in God as Abraham did would be counted as his seed. <u>Abraham believed in the resurrection of the dead.</u> But now that the true commands which are of that same faith have been established, and the actual resurrection of the true seed has occurred, we can no longer be justified before God through killing our children, or as the children of Israel, through conquering other countries, murdering, and burning up their land. In fact, this is denying Christ, because the covenant of faith is against it. It was through attacking the people that inhabited the land of promise before the Jews settled there, wiping them off the face of the earth, that the literal seed of Abraham under Joshua (after the first seed under Moses fell short) said by their actions that they believed in the promise of God to Abraham, that God would give them the land. But these things were but commandments of faith given for that day, until the day came that the true faith came through Jesus Christ. And the sequence of events was done and recorded to show us what would happen spiritually.

===========

The works were finished from the foundation of

the world. This speaks of a hard to accept truth. It seems to take away the idea that we have a choice, or are in control of our own destiny. Are you in control of <u>when</u> you were born? Or how you were made physically? *Romans 9:9 For this is the word of promise:* (the word of promise because God spoke here according to what He said to Abraham before, that He would give him a seed that would inherit the land.) *At this time will I come, and Sarah shall have a son.* Paul quotes here from *Genesis 18:10,* where in all actuality God says: *I will certainly return unto thee according to the time of life and lo, Sarah thy wife shall have a son.* Paul rewords the Old Testament scripture because the <u>time of life</u>, the seventh day, was during his time. Or was it the first? Or maybe the first and the last, the Alpha and Omega. Anyway, He was speaking of the birth of Isaac, to whom life was promised *(according to the time of life),* before he was even born. Isaac was predestined to be born on that day, and it was promised him that he would inherit the land before he was even created or did anything for it, as it was also Jacob: *Romans 9:10 And not only, but when Rebecca also had conceived 9:12 it was said unto her* by God about her children, *the elder,* Esau, *shall serve the younger,* Jacob. *As it is written: Jacob I have loved, but Esau have I hated.* This was said by God concerning the children before they were born, *9:11 For the children being not yet born, neither having done any good or evil so that the purpose of God might stand.* And because faith is required to get the promises, then how they were, their faith, and what they did were destined to be by God and created by God. And the events such as Jacob stealing the birthright of Esau were predestined to happen. If this is the case, then Esau's failure was determined by God, *Rom.9:14 what shall we say then, is there unrighteousness with God?* (I must say that if there was any other way of understanding these scriptures that I just went through then why else would God be thought of as unrighteous?) How could God do such a thing as determine one to fail and to wrath? God's answer is that He doesn't need your approval for what he does *9:15 For He saith to Moses, "I will have mercy and compassion on whom I want."* And, *9:18* says it very plainly to the point of undeniability (though it is still denied): *Therefore He has mercy on whom He wants, and to whom He will He hardens. 9:19 thou wilt say to me then, "Why does He yet find fault? For who has resisted His will?"* I mean, why would He condemn them then, and send them to hell forever if he is the one who hardened them? Paul doesn't give a very good answer except to say that we shouldn't question in the first place, *9:20 Nay, O man* (implying that we aren't anything but lowlife humans), *who art thou that replies against God? Shall the thing formed say to him that formed, "Why have you made me like this?"* Should you, being evil, ask God why He made you evil? Bet your saying yeah, huh? But even so, don't deny the truth that He did it as it says plainly again in *9:21–22 Hasn't the potter,* God, *power over the clay,* us, *of the same lump to make one vessel* *unto honor, <u>and another unto dishonor</u>? What if God endured with much longsuffering the vessels of wrath <u>fitted to destruction</u>,* the vessels created to be destroyed? So what is the reason for all this? Paul gives it in *9:23 that He might <u>make known the riches of His glory</u> on the vessels of mercy, which He had afore prepared,* before they were born, *unto glory.* And in *9:17 For the scripture says to Pharaoh,* who we know that he was the physical example of: *For this same purpose,* for this reason, *I have raised thee up: that I might show my power in thee.*

═══════════════

What if God endured with much longsuffering the vessels of wrath, that He might show us power, and make known the riches of His glory? So how does evil show God's power? And how does evil make known God's riches? What are the riches of God? His riches are love, mercy, gratefulness, joy, humility, life, hope, peace, tenderness, kindness, wisdom, understanding, etc. <u>God's purpose for all things is that we might know Him</u>. How are we going to know who God is unless He shows us? And how can he show us unless there is something to show us on? For example, we cannot be grateful to God unless He delivers us, and He cannot deliver us unless there is a pharaoh to deliver us from. And the greater the pharaoh, or evil that He delivers us from, the greater the gratitude and joy that He delivered us. But we cannot rejoice in God's power, glory, if He doesn't show us His power. And we cannot rejoice in God if we ourselves are strong enough to deliver us. The way God shows His power is by making something to bring us out of, or an opposite. If there was no enemy to defeat, then we wouldn't know God and His ability. The greater the power of the enemy created, the more we understand how powerful God is. And the greater the darkness, or lack of understanding that we have been in, the more we understand what light is. When we understand God, His ability, and his personality, then he creates in us His riches, His fruits, and Himself. And we stand in awe. And when we understand His mercy on us and all the things He has given us, we begin to love him and honor him for who and what He is. We could not understand what God is unless He showed us, "This is what I am not." And we would not respect Him, nor understand His mercy on us as much, or the things which He has given us unless he didn't give them to someone else. The greater the damnation on another, the greater the mercy on us, especially if we are the same way, if we are *of the same lump*. And because we are not saved because we did anything for it or are any better, *Romans 9:11: the purpose of God according to election might stand, not of works*. In this way humility is created, and gratitude is magnified. If you were never evil, God could never be merciful to you. Also, when you understand what God is not, then you understand what He is. The ultimate in understanding comes through experiencing things. I can know the poverty of another country, but when I go over the sea and experience it and then come back, there is gratefulness and joy. And I understand what I have—the peace. I could have always had peace but never known or understood it because I never experienced stress. What a waste. I could always have been with God as Adam, but would have never understood what I had; I would never <u>know</u> or understand life. It would be as if I was, not. It is kind of like if everything was white you wouldn't know what white was. But when black enters the scene, you would say, "Oh, that's white." In the same way, we know and understand love when hate and pain enters the scene, after we are taken away from it. I could always have had God, without ever being taken away from Him, but would never understand what I have, or know what I have. ***For in the day that ye eat of this fruit, ye shall be as Gods, knowing good and evil.*** I cannot be a being in and of myself unless I am separated from God; I would just be a robot. But I cannot be unless I am with God, because He is life. So I must be one and separate from God through experiencing death. When I get back to my country then, I will be alive in and of myself (who is myself?), and understand and appreciate what I have. I will know . . . <u>I AM</u>.

Isaiah 45:7 I form the light and create darkness: I make peace, and create evil: I the Lord do these things. Ever wonder why you don't hunt down and eat rats as a cat? Jesus said in ***Luke 11:40 Didn't He that made that which is without, also make that which***

is within? So if a non-Christian person has desires that we don't, is it smart to think ourselves better, or despise them, or to demand justice? Remember how you are in God's eyes. If evil was created for me that I may feel the pleasure of gratefulness, love, joy, know God's power, and understand what I have eternally among other reasons, then I owe it to them to be merciful to them. If a person is hardened against me for me, then I should still bless them . . . though they persecute me. And if God created them to be evil, and sees where they are going, is it wrong that they prosper in this world or get away with a lot? Or would we think that it is wrong that they didn't? If we cannot control our anger, then why do we get mad if another can't control the way they are? Maybe God feels sorry for them and so is merciful to them also in this short life. After all, He did create them, and there is nothing that doesn't do God's will in one way or another. Anger should not be in my vocabulary if all events are in God's hand, from the traffic jam to the lady who takes fifteen minutes at the cash register to pay. Jesus said the very hairs on your head are all numbered. Maybe in justice He is hard on those who are going to be with Him, knowing that we deserve it no more than they. It is hard to remember all this though when someone just hit you in the mouth. What we do to others will be done to us, believe that. Do you think that anything really offends God as we are offended, that He should take vengeance? Does God really take out evil for <u>His name's sake</u> as He often says in the scriptures if he has allowed evil to

Re-bek'ah

25

reign in the church for so long? Is He proud? Or does He do it for His names sake . . . for us, that we may not be proud?

———————————

Romans 9:9 *At this time will I come, and Sarah shall have a son.* So then, during Paul's time Sarah had a son, Isaac. Who is Sarah? Abraham's wife. Who is Abraham? The first Jew. God swore to Abraham that to him and his son, Isaac, He would give the promised land, and that He would multiply his son as the stars of the heaven, and as the sand of the sea. But this was all the physical example of the real and spiritual. Abraham was the example of God, and Isaac represented that true Son. Sarah represents what we are born by (God's covenant), as does Hagar, who was Sarah's servant and maid. She also gave birth by Abraham first, before Sarah did, to a son named Ishmael. Ishmael was born out of wedlock, of fornication and sin, to a mother who was in bondage. This was a representation of God's children who are wicked and disobedient, created through the Law of Moses. Am I just saying this? ***Galatians 4:21 don't you understand the law? For it is written, that Abraham had two sons, the one by a bondmaid,*** Hagar, ***the other by a freewoman,*** Sarah. ***4:23 He who was of the bondwoman was born after the flesh,*** <u>flesh</u> meaning literal, or natural, carnal, which is all sinful and wicked. So when Paul says flesh he is talking about things that are sinful. *But he* who was born *of the freewoman was by promise. 4:24 <u>Which things are an allegory</u>, for these* two women *are the two covenants; the one from mount Sinai,* where the covenant handed down through Moses came from, *which genders to bondage, which is Hagar.* Now catch this, <u>look</u>: *4:25 For this Hagar <u>is</u> Mt. Sinai, and answers to Jerusalem which now is, and is in bondage with her children. 4:26 But Jerusalem,* (so there are two Jerusalems), *which is above,* the heavenly, *is free, which is the mother of us all.* And she sits on Mt. Zion. So in the time of Paul was born the children of Sarah, and they her children as it says: *4:31 So then, brethren, we are not children of the bondwoman, but of the free.* And again in *4:28 now we brethren, as Isaac was, are the children of promise.* Look at *4:30 Cast out the bondwoman and her son, for the son of the bondwoman shall not be heir with the son of the free.* This will happen shortly, as Satan was cast out then. Because look further in *Romans 9:10.* It says that Isaac and Rebecca (or as the Old Testament puts it, <u>Re-bek'ah</u>), also had a child who was born of that same promise whose name was Jacob. But Isaac also had a firstborn son named Esau, who gave up his birthright to Jacob. If the generation of Paul was Isaac, *(we then, as Isaac was, are the children of promise),* and Isaac had two sons, the firstborn being Esau, then isn't it time for Jacob? Both sons were born of the same mother, of one covenant, Rebecca, which was handed down by

Jesus Christ. Nevertheless, only one son was of promise. It is time for the younger, us, to take Esau's birthright.

========

Some doubts and questions have arisen about <u>legalism.</u> A wicked term indeed. You caught me, I need to make it clear that I am indeed preaching <u>for</u> the law, the commandments of Jesus Christ, not against it, and that strict (but not excessive) obedience is a must, though it's not. Hear me out now. Taken from the same verse: ***Galatians 4:21 Tell me, you that desire to be under the law, do you not understand the law? For it is written:*** Hmmm. In the following verses, all the way to the end of the chapter and beyond, (the verses that Paul is calling <u>the law</u> in *4:21*), is not written a single commandment. Now if Paul were trying to explain literally the law (commandments), where is one written in the following verses? If he were talking about the Law of Moses (or Jesus' commandments or laws for that matter), why aren't they written here? Aren't the verses that Paul is quoting following *4:21,* which he is calling the law in *4:21,* taken from the book of Genesis? And one verse, twenty-seven, from Isaiah? So when Paul speaks of the law he is not always talking about commandments, whether Moses' or Christ's. But almost always <u>he is talking about all the books of the Old Testament, and the entire covenant handed down by Moses, not just</u>

the ten commandments. Before the New Testament was added to the bible, there was just the old, divided into four sections called The Law, The Prophets, Wisdom, and some other book I forgot. Rarely does Paul call the covenant handed down by Christ a law, even though in His covenant there are laws. Some of these laws are the same as Moses' and are necessary to keep, such as in the Ten Commandments. Some laws are indeed completely the opposite of Moses'. But most of Jesus' commandments do not contradict Moses' at all. Most of Moses' laws are no longer necessary to keep literally because in Christ we fulfill them spiritually. But we still <u>must fulfill them</u> in order to be free from them. When you're under Christ's law there is no law. Christ's covenant is and isn't a law. When you are under the Law of Moses, or any law including Christ's, you are in sin: ***Romans 4:15 Because the law works wrath, for where no law is, there is no transgression***. If there was no law that said, "Thou shalt wear a seatbelt," then I wouldn't be disobeying it when I didn't. Because I have sin in me I will sin eventually and so die. So if you are under the law you are in sin because ***1John 3:4*** says ***sin is the transgression of the law. Romans 3:9 They are all in sin,*** Jews and Gentiles, ***3:10 there is none righteous, no not one. 3:11 there is none that understand. 3:18 there is no fear of God before their eyes. 3:13 with their tongues they have deceived.*** Now again in ***3:19*** of this New Testament book Paul is talking about ***Romans 3:10–18*** that he just quoted from the Old Testament prophets, including David's writings in the book of Psalms. In ***3:10–18*** is not written a single commandment. So when Paul says in *3:19 now we know that whatever things <u>the law</u> says, it says to them that are under the law, (so that every mouth may be stopped),* he is not talking about the law of Christ, the righteousness of God as he calls it in *3:20–26.* And in that he is speaking in *3:20–26* of two laws it says plainly in *3:27 where is boasting then? It is excluded. By what law? Of works? No, but by <u>the law of faith.</u>* Here he says that there are two laws, or covenants. One of faith, which Christ handed down, in which there is no law. And the other of works, handed down by Moses.

———————————

Galatians 2:16 We know that a man is not justified by the works of the law, but by the faith of Jesus Christ. What <u>works of the law</u> was Paul talking about? Look in the verses written before. Peter, an Apostle of Jesus, was convinced by Jesus that it was okay to eat with people who were not Jews *(Acts 10),* and did so even though it was against the Law of Moses: *Galatians 2:12 he did eat with the gentiles.* But when the Gentiles came to Peter, instead of Peter going to them, he would not eat with them in front of the Jews. He was afraid that the Jews would stone him or something for disobeying the law: *2:12 But when they were come, he withdrew and separated himself, fearing them that were of the circumcision.* Now I imagine that this action of Peter's hurt the Gentiles' feelings a bit, embarrassed them, and offended them. That just because they were not of a certain race they were considered altogether filthy dogs, unworthy even to eat with. This was the Law of Moses, which commanded that a Jew was not to eat with Gentiles. A Gentile is anyone who is not a Jew. All Jews were circumcised, Gentiles weren't. And when you continue to do the works of the Law of Moses (which in this case is sin because Jesus says otherwise), you are not believing in Jesus. You have not stopped doing your old works . . . the law. When you don't believe in Jesus, you are saying that God's word, His promise given to Abraham is not true (because God promised that He would send His Son, raise Him from the dead, and give a new covenant by Him). Paul didn't like that Peter and the people with him denied the Truth by doing this to the Gentiles, by sinning against Christ: *2:14 But when I saw that they walked not uprightly according to the truth of the gospel, 2:11 I withstood him,* (Peter), *to the face because he was to be blamed. 2:16 A man is not justified by the works of the law, but by the faith of Jesus Christ.* So am I saying that we are justified originally by our actions? Nope. I say that because God is merciful to our actions, we believe the Truth, Jesus, that Word spoken to us. Through that faith are we righteous in God's eyes. Then we are made one with God, perfected, through obedience to the covenant of faith, not Moses'. This is done by the Spirit of Jesus, not us. Look at *Galatians 3:3 having begun in the Spirit, are you now made perfect by the flesh?* So this says that these Galatians are believers, and are already in the Spirit, so these verses are speaking to believers. I don't like the fact that verse sixteen seems to say that you are made right with God by what you do; that is easy to agree with, right? So what if I said *2:16 We have believed in Jesus Christ,* (in our mind, not actions, and are justified by that), *that we might be perfected by the faith of Christ,* the law of Christ. I think it good that when these words are used, to use both justified and perfected.

Galatians 2:16 For by the works of the law shall no flesh be justified. A person must be perfect in God's eyes to be justified, and no one was until Christ came, though they still had Him. *Hebrews 11:39* says *And these all,* speaking about people of faith in the Old Testament, *received not the promise, 11:40 God having provided some better thing for us, that without us they should not be made perfect.* They were servants, not sons. But even while we are sons we are not completely perfect until we die, (until we know the only I am), though we are. *Galatians 2:17 But if, while we seek to be justified by Christ, we ourselves also are found sinners, is Christ the minister of sin?* This verse, as with many verses, has several meanings. Moses' covenant bred, or administered sin and death as says *2 Corinthians 3:7 But if the ministration of death, written and engraven in stones . . .* and again in *2:9 For if the ministration of condemnation be glorious . . .* So

Paul asks in *Galatians 2:17* if Christ also ministered sin. (And in that you can be found a sinner under Christ it says *But if we ourselves also,* as were the Jews under Moses, *are found sinners.* So there is that possibility). But, *Is Christ* in us *the servant of sin? God forbid!* But who is myself? Or in the case of being found a sinner, <u>was</u>? *2:18 For if I build again the things which I destroyed, I make <u>myself</u> a transgressor.* Did I myself destroy anything, or did Christ when I was saved? Is He my savior, or am I? And if I, my soul, is dead, *2:19 For I through the law <u>am dead</u> to the law,* who is the other I? *Romans 7:18* answers: *For I know that in me, (that is, in my flesh), dwells no good thing. 7:15 For that which I do, I allow not.* So there are two <u>me's</u> in my flesh (my physical body), besides my soul, which is dead. Christ took my old life that was one with my soul, (me), and put it in him up in heaven. So now I have this other life, which is also Christ, that is one with me, (my soul and body), because it is here with me. But it is not one with me because in me it is a separate being than me my soul and body. Christ divided my soul and spirit, and so in this way I my soul is dead because my spirit was my life. Nevertheless, I my soul is alive because there is a new Life in this physical body . . . which also is Christ. But there is another me, sin, still here with me my soul in this body which is not in me because it is separate from my soul. Christ crucified it. When Christ entered me He took my old life, which was one with sin, and took us to hell. God raised Himself from the dead in me and put the old me, now cleansed from sin (my life rather), in Him up there, and so separated me from sin. And put himself in my body. *Colossians 3:3 For you are dead, and your life is hid with Christ in God. 3:4 When Christ, who is our life . . .* Back to *Galatians 2:20 I am crucified with Christ, nevertheless I live, yet not I, but <u>Christ</u> lives in me, and the life which <u>I</u> now live . . .* Didn't he just get through saying he <u>didn't</u> live? Then who is the "I" that now lives? *I live by the faith of the Son of God.* I am totally at the mercy of God whether I will walk in faith. I do not save myself, or make myself; He does by His mercy and <u>by the faith that He has</u> as it also says, *I live by the faith of the Son of God.*

=====

Galatians 2:19 For I through the law am dead to the law, I am crucified with Christ. So as long as I am under the Law of Christ, I am not under the Law of Moses and of Christ, because the only law I was crucified under was the faith, right? I was not crucified under the Law of Moses. So when Paul says, *I through the <u>law</u> am dead,* he must be talking about Jesus' commandments of faith. And if I am crucified then I am dead, and if I am dead then I am not in this world, so it cannot be me who is living by faith. *2:20 nevertheless I live; yet not I, but Christ lives the life which <u>I</u> now live in the flesh by the faith.* So I shouldn't be proud. I am not strong enough to turn from sin. If I was, I would not need Jesus. I would be my own savior, and there would be no need for Christ to have died: *2:21 I do not frustrate the grace of God.* And if I could keep the commandments of Moses, or if it were necessary to, and were justified under that law, then Christ died for no reason: *for if righteousness come by the law, then Christ is dead in vain.* Because a savior would not be sent by God unless you needed saving. So then I should not keep doing the works of the Law of Moses, but should believe in Jesus Christ. *Galatians 3:10 For as many as are of the works of the law,* that continue to live under sin, *are under the curse. For it is written, Cursed is everyone that continues not in all things which are written in the book of the law to do them.* And the book of the law witnessed the covenant that was to come under Christ, that we would be made right with God through faith in Him and not through itself: *3:11 That no man is justified by the law in the sight of God is evident, for* the book of the law says *the just shall live by faith. 3:12 And the law is not of faith.* We do the Law of Moses, we continue in it and fulfill it by believing in Christ. The book of the law says in *3:12 The man that does them,* (the law), *shall live in them.* But we don't keep its commandments literally, or naturally. We don't live in the flesh, but we keep them spiritually, in Spirit and in Truth. Because the Old Testament has hidden spiritual meaning that is unveiled in the gospel of Jesus Christ: *ROMANS 1:17 For therein,* (in the gospel as it says in *1:16*), *is the righteousness of God revealed,* made <u>known</u> or <u>shown</u>. One reason that the gospel reveals the righteousness of God is that God spoke before in the Old Testament writings that these events would take place. Not only did he say it, but He swore with an oath that He would fulfill these words spoken, or these hidden truths. When God did these things through Christ, (fulfilled them), then He made Himself true because His words were found to be true. So when we say that Jesus is true, when we believe in Jesus, we say God's word is true and that God is righteous. If we don't believe in the word of God, the truth, the gospel, then we say that God is a liar. But when the beginning of verse seventeen says that in the gospel *the righteousness of God is revealed,* it also means the gospel's commandments given by Jesus. *1:16 the gospel of Christ is the power of God unto salvation because therein is the righteousness of God made known.* The New Testament reveals the entire covenant with the commandments of God given by Jesus, which are different than the Law of Moses. When we obey these commandments, we are saying by our actions that we really believe that Jesus was the one promised by God that He would establish a covenant with which would give us eternal life. So when we hear the truth of the gospel and believe it that is faith, *1:17 from faith,* and when we do the commandments written therein that faith materializes *to faith. As it is written, the just shall live by faith.* So then, those who act righteously will walk in faith, *1:18 because against those who hold,* who have, *the truth in unrighteousness the wrath of God is revealed.* The curse.

Romans 1:18 For the wrath of God is revealed from heaven against all who hold the truth in unrighteousness. 1:19 Because that which may be <u>known</u> of God, His truth, His word, *is <u>manifest in them,</u> for God hath showed it unto them.* Here it is saying plainly that God has been manifested inside them. Look at verse twenty-one: *Because that when they <u>knew God.</u>* <u>When we believe something we accept it within us as true.</u> When we believe that word, the word gets manifested in us. We become one with it. We <u>know</u> it. Just as physically we can marry and become one with the opposite sex. (Rather, when we hear the word and it chooses to make itself known we believe it.) Regardless, *1:20 because the invisible things of him from the creation of the world,* that is, the secret truths of his word hidden in the scriptures, *are clearly seen, being understood by the things that are made, his eternal power and Godhead.* Jesus Christ is the head of the body and God's power is in His Truth. *So that they are without excuse,* because they can't say they didn't know. The wrath of God comes *Romans 1:21 Because when they knew God, they glorified Him not as God.* To <u>glorify</u> in this respect means to bring honor to. When we call ourselves Christian, when we say that we have Christ in us, and then live in sin, we say that Christ is a sinner. "Ah yes, Jesus lives in me, He is my savior," he says as he snorts a line of cocaine and molests a little boy. *1:21* (They) *became vain in their imaginations and their foolish heart was darkened.* How can something be darkened unless it is first brought to light? Can a candle be blown out if it is not lit? Hasn't your heart and mind, your spirit, been enlightened by God's words? <u>Light is spiritual understanding</u>. It is God's power. Sure you want to know Him? If so, may I suggest (strongly), that you seek after Him with all your heart? Find out all you can once you get started and walk humbly: *1:22 Professing themselves to be wise,* like some great teacher of God, *they became fools. 1:23 And changed the glory of the <u>uncorruptible</u> God into an image made like to corruptible man.* Christ is the image and glory of God. *1:25 <u>who changed the Truth of God into a lie.</u>* The curse of God is upon a person who denies the truth, who says by their actions that God is a liar, because they say His Word is not true after having accepted it. Since God cannot lie, they make <u>themselves</u> a liar. *Romans 1:24 therefore <u>God also gave them up</u> to uncleanness through the lusts of their heart.* Again in *1:26 For this cause God <u>gave them up</u> unto vile affections.* Now again folks, you cannot give something up that you don't have first. Again in *1:28 And even as they did not like to retain God in knowledge, God <u>gave them over</u> to a reprobate mind.* So now instead of Christ, they have in them a sinful Christ that is not the real Jesus. They have a false Christ, an antichrist. Let's prove this. *1 John 2:4 He that says "I know Him," and keeps not His commandments, is a liar.* Hmmm. A <u>liar</u>. Look in *1 John 2:22: Who is a liar but he that denies that Jesus is Christ?* That doesn't keep his commandments? *<u>He is antichrist,</u>* who says they have Christ and doesn't keep his commandments. So with their mouth they confess Him, and in works they deny Him. As the book of *Titus* says in *1:16 they profess that they know God, but in*

Darrell Gilbert

38

works they deny Him. The antichrist is not one person but many, but those many make up one body. Just as Christ is not just one member, but many persons in one body. ***1 John 2:18 as ye have heard that antichrist shall come, even now are there many antichrists.*** Here it also states that the antichrist has already come. ***1John 1:6 If we say that we have fellowship with Him, and walk in darkness, we lie, and do not the truth.*** We do not <u>do the truth</u>. When we sin, we deny Christ. When we deny Christ, we lie, because we say that God's word is not true that He <u>swore</u> would happen. When we call God a liar we seriously oppose ourself, or Christ in us. God cannot lie, and he swore. He will not become a liar that we may remain true. So we make <u>ourself</u> a liar, we oppose ourself. We are against-ourself, anti-christ. The curse is that the thing that is in sin doesn't understand they are or will deny that they are. They really are in opposition with themselves. Bringing them out to the light is hard so he says: ***if we say that we have no sin, we deceive ourselves, and the truth is not in us*** any longer, because he has denied us. Although it was, it is not because God's word is true. He cannot lie. The truth is that ***Romans 3:23 all have sinned and come short of the glory of God. 1 John 1:10 If we say that we have not sinned, we make him a liar, and his word is not in us.*** (This is the beast in ***Revelations 17:8 that was and is not.*)

Rebecca

Doesn't history have a way of repeating itself? I will continue in the book of *Galatians 3:13 Christ has redeemed us from the curse of the law, being made a curse for us, for it is written: Cursed is everyone that hangs on a tree.* So the same curse was back before Christ came. But the curse that then was, was less severe than the one that was to come because the people that lived before Christ had not become <u>one</u> with God; they weren't <u>perfect</u>. They were servants, not Sons. Look at *Galatians 4:1 The heir, as long as he is a child, differs nothing from a servant, though he be lord of all, but is under tutors and governors until the time appointed of the father. 4:3 Even so we, when we were children, were in bondage under the elements of the world.* (The word element has a similar meaning to rudiment. They mean something that is in raw form, in this respect, <u>laws</u> of God. Something in the beginning stages of development, as of a plan. In biology the word means an undeveloped body part; embryo.) This will trip you out if you know what I know. Anyway, though people still had life, they were saved, yet with life they were undeveloped, as of a child. They were blind, not knowing what was going on. They were in darkness. They were still under the dominion of sin and death, under its law: *4:4 But when the fullness of the time was come, God sent forth his Son, 4:5 to set them free that were under the law,* under sin. *4:7 So you are no more a servant, but a Son. 4:8 But then,* that is, before Christ came, *when you <u>knew</u> not God, you did service to them,* angels, *which by nature are not gods.* In the same way, now there are those who are in the same state. They may believe something that isn't true and even teach it in ignorance, they may have sinned and definitely haven't been holy, but God is merciful and knows the hearts. He has not denied us, nor utterly forgotten about us, but has remembered His promise to us. And so the Lord has now said, *"Thou art my Son, Today I have begotten thee" (Hebrews 5:5).* So this scripture then is the gospel. <u>Jesus Christ died and rose again</u>, because in order for Him to be begotten, He would have to have been dead. Those that hear the truth and accept it, who repent and believe the gospel, are and will be saved. But those who deny that they have sinned, who continue speaking lies, are condemned already, because he has not believed. Once again in *Galatians 3:22 the scripture has concluded all under sin,* because the death of Christ on the cross foretold in an <u>elemental</u> way what would happen spiritually <u>within us</u>. That Christ would be betrayed by that son of perdition of whom Judas Iscariot was the example of. Jesus says to God in *John 17:22 Those that thou has given me I have kept, and have lost none <u>but</u> the <u>Son</u> of perdition.* Who was Judas? Wasn't he one of the twelve Apostles chosen of God? A priest of Jesus? Didn't he turn against Christ for money? *(Luke 22:3–5).* And because of these Judas's, Christ would be crucified within us as told in **Hebrews 6:6 If they shall fall away, they crucify to themselves the Son of God again. 2 Thessalonians 2:3 Let no man deceive you, for that day,** (the coming of the Lord), **shall not come except there come a falling away first, and that man of sin be revealed, the <u>son</u> of perdition.** Wasn't Judas hung on a tree? **(Matthew 27:5).** And again, **"Cursed is everyone that hangs on a tree."** So then Judas represented that curse that he also would bring. Because the scripture foretold concerning Christ in **Luke 22:37** that **He was numbered among the transgressors.** So then Christ would be counted as a sinner before God. And Jesus said in **22:37 the things concerning me <u>have an end</u>.** And again in **Matthew 26:31 I will smite the shepherd, and the sheep will be scattered.** And again when Christ was on the cross He said **My God, my God, why hast thou forsaken me?** More characteristic of Judas is that he pretends like he loves Jesus, **Luke 22:48 Judas, betrayest thou the Son of man with a kiss?** And **Luke 22:23–27** speaks right after talking about Judas that His betrayer would love to be in the highest positions, lifted up with pride, as a preacher. **John 13** also speaks the same, that they like to be served rather than to serve, that they are great in this world and not lowly. The Lord has also said concerning that antichrist in **Luke 22:21 Behold, the hand of him that does betray me is with me at the table.** As it is written, **John 13:18 He that eats bread with me has lifted up his heel against me.** So then those who fellowship with us, who eat the same bread, that word of God, have betrayed us. And Jacob was born on the heel of Esau. I have so much to say but I have to go to work. This is what I say, that Christ has died and rose again, that this is the third day, the second 7th. *Galatians 3:23 before faith came, we were kept under the law, shut up unto the faith that should afterwards be revealed.* This then is the revealing of the faith that was done literally in the time of Christ. <u>Jesus Christ died and rose again</u>.

Look at *Luke 22:35–38* closely and consider. If Jesus were really giving commandments for them to do at that time, and were speaking about literal swords for them to use at that time, why then in *22:51* did He tell them not to use the swords they bought? So if He were commanding and speaking in *22:37* of events that were about to happen only literally, and immediately, then He would not have healed the servant's ear.

==========

Tom,

Do you know what has happened? I have said that the church now is Esau. *Deuteronomy 13:6 If thy brother,* (Esau), *the son of thy mother,* (the covenant of Jesus Christ), *which is as thine own soul, entice thee secretly saying "let us go and serve other Gods"* or as in *13:5 has spoken to turn you away from the Lord* (this is done through false beliefs . . .

secretly). *13:8 Thou shalt not consent unto him, nor listen to him. Neither shall thine eye,* (what you see with, your Spirit), *pity him nor spare him, nor will you conceal him,* (He must be made known). *13:9 But thou shalt surely kill him. Thine hand shall be first upon him to put him to death, thou shalt stone him.* The Word of God is that stone. *13:11 And all Israel shall hear, and fear, and shall do no more such wickedness. So shalt thou put away evil from <u>the midst of thee.</u>* I have said that <u>Wicked</u> will be cast out shortly. *2 Thessalonians 2:8 And then shall that <u>Wicked</u> be made known . . . whom the Lord shall consume with the Spirit of His mouth.* Know for absolutely certain that this will happen shortly as with you, but to some the Lord will harden and not show mercy. And to others he will show mercy; they will see the truth as you did in my first letters, and then He will allow Satan to blind them and they will immediately forget all that was shown to them . . . as he has shown you can be done, even now. I wonder a lot about what you are thinking and how you are. Am I now going to be considered "beside myself"? I feel like we need to make sure that we know that what we are teaching out of the bible is true. The worse thing a person can do is continue to teach something false, or that he is unsure is true about God, especially after the Lord has chastened Him for it. I want to communicate with you, and discuss the bible and our beliefs, even if it's just by e-mail, because I suspect the Lord will never let you go, and that He loves you very much. *Deuteronomy 11 Know ye this, for I*

speak not with your children which have not known the chastisement of the Lord, his miracles, his acts, and his mighty hand. But your eyes have seen all the great acts of the Lord which He did, therefore shall ye keep all the commandments, that ye may prolong your days in the land which the Lord sware unto your fathers to give unto their seed. Let me know how ya are (whether I am crazy or not to you), and maybe some verses we can talk about? *Peace be unto you,*
    Darrell

══════════════

Romans 2:17 Behold, thou art called a Jew, and rests in the law. Now if you will think about that verse for a second, you might understand something secret. If you understand what I am talking about, don't worry, you're not under the law, because you are not asleep. If you were, you wouldn't understand. So if you don't understand what I am saying this verse is true to you, but then you wouldn't understand that you didn't understand, even if I told you. And to those who do understand, it is yet true to us because we are not with Christ fully. And maybe if you don't understand you are just not perfect yet, who am I to say. I find it absolutely amazing . . . scary, but awesomely amazing how a person can say so plainly the Truths of God to another with strong assurance, and the person doesn't understand or still denies the truth. And doesn't understand that they don't understand. Something else I consider extremely frightening when I really understand is that I know without doubt that these people who wrote these books fully understood these things and yet some "forgot" them because they turned from God. They did not know that they fell asleep either. *John 12:35 For He who walks in darkness knows not where he is going.* When I understand, it makes me get on my knees in astonishment, with tears, begging God to forgive me and thanking Him for it. Do trust me please that there is an extremely precious reward, beyond the word precious, precious reward to those who are strictly obedient to God. That reward makes you all the more diligent to keep His commandments because you know the importance of it. The commandments of Christ are no different than yesterday, or the day before for that matter, although hidden then. This day they are no different than when Christ told them by His Apostles, because they were revealed in spiritual form. They are the same, and so is the covenant of faith, even before Christ. I said to myself after our bible study on Wednesday, "Man I hope they just haven't gotten around to reading my e-mails, maybe that's why they are saying what they are." Kind of frustrating, but I have to have the attitude for my own sanity, and so that I will continue to write, that if they hear they hear, and if they don't they don't. Truly it is all in God's hands. *1 Corinthians 15:34 Awake to righteousness and sin not, for some have not the*

Darrell Gilbert

knowledge of God.

I want to say that I know that you know a lot of the stuff that I will go through. I speak as if to an idiot because I plan on printing out the stuff that I write and making booklets out of it. I realize that not everyone has a computer, so the e-mails that I sent out before I took all the names and e-mail addresses out of except mine, made a booklet, and am passing it out to various churches and people freely. I give my e-mail address and let them know that I want them to e-mail me if they want more, but they never do even though the scripture says *Thou shalt not muzzle the ox that treads out the corn.* I want you to know also that although I do hand out booklets and will indeed spread my beliefs in this way, I am not looking to take over the class or anyone's church, that should be obvious by now. For this reason (among others), I have made a commitment to just <u>write</u>. I will not lead a bible study in this church or any other, nor will I take a podium even if asked. I will rarely if ever speak face to face with anyone about God. Something bad always happens when I do these things, or something always happens that keeps me from doing them. I have also come to the conclusion that I should visit other churches and spread the gospel by handing out books to them so I don't know how much I will be around. The job of preaching the gospel doesn't always make for companionship, and teaching about God is NOT the way to pick up chics! I know that there are some that think I am stupid because I don't make a book and sell it, but there is just something about selling Jesus for money that doesn't sound appealing to me.* I don't condemn others at all for it, because God has said in *1 Corinthians 9:9 Thou shalt not muzzle the ox that treadeth out the corn.* (I feel the Lord has made me as an ox, to be used by Jesus to plow up the hardened ground of the land of Israel so that they may bring forth fruit to God.) But God has blessed me with a job that I may profit more in heaven by freely giving the gift that was freely given to me. And this job can easily be transferred from place to place, even throughout the world. So I would not accept money from anyone either, even if asked. My business is called "Furnitureworks." The Lord has blessed me with the wisdom and a unique ability to fix defects in wood, to beautify it and to make it more durable. And the Lord's house needs pretty furniture, don't 'cha think? I know that there are some people that will try to use what I teach for their own glory, and for this reason they think me a fool to speak it to anyone, especially other teachers. But I happen to believe that there is nothing that a person can do, nor is there anything that a person can receive that is more than what God gives to Him. And no person ever truly gives birth without first going through labor pains. I know everyone knows my reputation as a failure. Truly I am, and will tell a person to this day that I have failed God more than anyone. It's because I think that you all are more deserving of God's blessings than me, I share what I know with you. But I have been a Christian for twelve years, not just the one that this church has known me, and no one knows the hell I have been put through and have remained faithful in before my fall. I really appreciate the respect and carefulness taken by everyone thus far not to offend me in this respect. When I am strong though, I happen to get great joy out of hearing others share in their own words what God may have taught them. And if they quote me outright, to just say, "A certain other person besides me once wrote," or something similar would be very acceptable. I believe it when Jesus said in my favorite parable of the bible *Luke 14:11 He that exalts himself shall be humbled, and he that humbles himself shall be exalted.* Because God knows that I am slammed and humiliated openly by Jesus on a regular basis. And when it all comes down to it, God knows who did what and is the one who gives it anyway, and will reward me. When I understand this, why do I try so hard to win souls over another? No matter how much I try, I will get no more than what is appointed me. So everyone should just take a chill pill, and give glory to others. Truly in giving we receive. So this is why I do what I do.

*footnote: Obviously, I changed my mind. The reason for this is the ease and quickness of getting the word out nationwide with the assurance that it is being spread in it's entirety, and without another person claiming to be something they aren't or watering it down. Also the huge church that had the capability of spreading this doctrine nationwide, which originally received it with great enthusiasm and began to do so, eventually rejected me. So this is the way that

I decided to do it myself.

———————————

Imagine a circle. This is Jesus. In that circle imagine another smaller circle. This is God the Father. God <u>in</u> Christ (being a separate thing, but <u>in</u> Jesus), created all things. So <u>only</u> God the Father created all things. So Jesus Christ created all things including me because God did it in Him. Now split the small circle that is within the big circle into two semicircles, yet keep the two halves together. (This is the best way I know how to explain something that in all actuality is one thing.) The Father, unlike Jesus when He created all things, has always had Life in Himself—the Spirit. (Do not imagine a circle within a circle when it comes to the Father and the Spirit, because they are one.) The Father and the Spirit have always been <u>completely</u> one. Imagine now another big circle totally separate from all the other circles, split it in half with both the semicircles together. This is the Father. So the Father was not in Christ when He created all things but was a separate being, so the Spirit Himself alone in Christ created all things. So Jesus Himself alone (the first big circle), created all things without the Father, the other big circle.

Before anything was ever made, Jesus was, and Jesus created all of us. But Jesus was created by the Father: ***Colossians 1:15 who is the beginning, <u>the</u>***

firstborn of every creature. And in that this verse is not speaking of the now, it says in **1:18** (Christ is) **_the firstborn from the dead._** So Christ was, and is. No other thing created by God has life to this day except Jesus. He is still the only begotten Son of God. So Jesus said, **_"Before Abraham was, I am."_** And by Him all things are being created again, including a new world, except truly by Him alone this time. He alone is God. He said it as a prophecy. And truly when He said it, He was, because He also was the first perfected. And He was before Abraham, because He was before all, and created all. **_Colossians 1:17 He is_** (alive) **_before all things._** So you could say that God created Himself. But the Father has given birth to a wholly separate being than Himself, His Son, as He has always been with the Spirit, with Jesus. So Jesus has always been. Has the Father always been? **_Colossians 1:15 Who_** (Jesus) **_is the image of the invisible God._** Look at yourself. Jesus was as your physical body is to your soul and spirit (only not physical, but unseen). Because though your outward body and your inward body are one, they are also separate things, right? Because if you were to die, your soul would still be. This is an example of how Jesus was before He came here, as well as we ourselves. Though we were, we were not, because we ourselves did not have life in and of ourself. And we were created in an order, and by some others were. **_John 1:1 In the beginning,_** Jesus (the original circle), **_was the Word,_** the Spirit within that circle, **_And the Word,_** both circles as a whole, **_was with God,_** with

God (the other circle), because He was separate from that other circle, *and the Word was God,* because within the first circle He was that circle. Now imagine another circle around both the <u>big</u> circles (including the half circles within). This is the <u>beginning,</u> the Father, with the Son and the Spirit (both those circles) within Him. *In the beginning,* the Father, *was the Word,* Jesus Christ, *and the Word was with God,* the Spirit beside Him, *And the Word was God.* This keeps going within and without forever.

———————————

Okay, Okay. I will admit it. Not that I have at all lied about anything, but I want to tell the truth because I have come to the absolute certainty that there are two things on the top of God's list that He loves more than anything else . . . honesty and humility. I did, I did . . . I did fear that someone would use my doctrines for their own glory, and I was slow to speak for this reason. What drove me to tell you all at first more than anything else was not faith that I would be exalted in this life right now, but a reward in heaven. <u>Nor did I at all intend for the first letter or my actions to have the impact that I now see that it did.</u> Also, I just got to the point that I didn't care if someone used my glory, that you all deserve it more anyway. If it wasn't against my beliefs, I would <u>swear</u> to you this. I am not planning this stuff out nor am I at all this intelligent. I also am learning as I go. I love this. There is a sense of great freedom in humility and honesty. See, now I don't have to hold up to the standard of the previous letters. I am telling you that I can't. If I fail you or put you to shame, then it is me and I am sorry. God knows that I am a failure, really. If I am exalted, then believe me it is not because I meant to do it or planned it out. I didn't even understand what you got out of it until after you. I went to church wondering what everyone was upset over. I wasn't even going to add the letter to my booklet. And if anyone reads this letter and doesn't know what I am talking about, and thinks me a fool . . . then your right!! And guess what? I don't care! Ha! But I am confident that this church has experienced the power that I afterward did. Believe me that I feel great joy and love for you all. I am so happy that I have people to write to. I am truly very excited. And I am coming to the definite conclusion that God will **bruise Satan under our feet shortly.** Not to say that I won't be humbled, but I perceive that even when I lose that the Lord will turn it to victory through His awesome power. Whooooooaaaa!!!!

Some things are a sin for a human to speak and know. ***Thou shalt not discover thy father's skirt.*** What else can I do or say to get the doubting Thomas' to believe? I greatly wish all to believe in my heart. *2 Corinthians 11:16 Let no man think me a fool,* (please) . . . *yet as a fool receive me that I may boast a little.* I am talking on things that I heard on the radio from different people, in particularly a preacher of another church. I hope this letter gets to him. One of my favorite stories in the bible is the story of Jesus raising Lazarus from the grave in *John 11,* because truly this is how the Lord has dealt with me and the church, in particularly the preachers. We have been spiritually sick, that is, <u>asleep in darkness.</u> Due to our sins, our sickness, we cannot see the light but are in darkness. But to those Jesus loves much, he deals with them as in *11:5 Now Jesus loved Lazarus, 11:6 When he had heard therefore that he was sick, he abode two days still in the same place where he was.* Jesus just let him die completely, knowing that he was sick and about to die. This he did after He said that Lazarus would not die of his sickness in verse four. Probably because it was one day after Lazarus got sick that Jesus heard of his sickness, He stayed there two days that he may come to him on the third. He knew by then that his sin had taken him so he says to the twelve in verse eleven: *Our friend Lazarus sleeps, but I go that I may awake Him out of sleep.* And indeed Jesus went to the very people that hated Him before, *11:7 let us go into Judea again* (the land of the Jews). And the verses showing that Thomas, (us preachers), didn't understand at that time what He was saying or doing were written to tell us that the people who were really asleep were us, and that what He was doing to Lazarus was what He would do to us Thomas' spiritually. And truly your family members care to the point of tears, so as Mary pleaded, I also pray to Jesus, *11:32 Lord, if thou had been here, my brother* (Esau) *had not died.* I also

Darrell Gilbert

54

had no idea what he was doing to me. The mercy and love of our Lord be with you.

========================

Isaiah 28:11 For with stammering lips and another tongue will I speak to this people. God is speaking to me loud out of the book of *Isaiah 58:1 Cry aloud, spare not, lift up thy voice like a <u>trumpet</u>.* Truly, *1 Thessalonians 4:16 the trumpet shall sound, <u>the voice of an archangel</u>, and the dead in Christ shall rise.* I am trying to interpret as I go because Paul says in *1 Corinthians 14:8 For if the <u>trumpet</u> give an uncertain sound, who shall prepare himself to the battle?* But no matter what I say or how, truly to some it will be uncertain, because it is prophesied in *1 Corinthians 14:21* that some will choose not to believe; they will not hear the sound of the trumpet. Jesus said in *Luke 17:20, The Kingdom of God comes not with observation, 17:21 neither shall they say, "Look here!" or "Look there!" for the Kingdom of God is <u>within you</u>.* Although it will also come without on the 3rd last day. Again in *2 Peter 1:19 The daystar shall arise in your hearts.* I will say this: *2 Peter 3:8* though *a day is as a thousand years,* truly *<u>a thousand years is as a day</u> (Mark 4: 26–29).* I can only imagine what Paul felt like trying to convince the Jews of his day to turn from Hagar to Sarah. But there is no change in the law from Sarah to Rebecca. Although they are different covenants—we are born of different mothers—they are both of the same promise and of the same law. Neither covenant is sin, unless of course you deny your own mother Rebecca, then you deny both. *Galatians 3:25 But after that faith is come you are no longer under a schoolmaster.* Just as Sarah (the covenant of promise, who Isaac was born by) was around while Ishmael had dominion, Rebecca, my mother, was around while Isaac had dominion, because it was known and prophesied. And indeed Sarah is my grandmother but Hagar is not. Hagar is Esau's grandmother because Esau and Ishmael are under the same law, although given by different mothers. *Isaiah 28:22* says: *I have heard of the Lord God a <u>consumption</u>, even <u>determined</u> upon the whole earth.* Look in *Hebrews 12:29 For our God is a <u>consuming fire</u>.* Remember that Paul in the book of *Galatians 4:21–26* says that there are two mountains: mount Sinai, and mount Zion. Both of these are <u>Jerusalems</u> *(vs. 25&26).* These mounts represent His children, or cities where His people dwell and live in. The women that sat on them, Hagar and Sarah, represent the laws or covenants, what we are <u>born</u> by. PLEEEEEASE take the time to read *Exodus ch. 19 &20.* When the Lord came down from heaven he <u>consumed</u> with the fire of His word that first mount, Sinai. *Exodus 19:10 The Lord said to Moses, Go unto the people, and sanctify them today,* during his time, *tomorrow,* the time of Christ, *and let them*

***wash their clothes and be ready against the third
day, for the third day the Lord will come down in
the sight of all the people upon Mt. Sinai. 10:16
And it came to pass on the third day in the morning
that there were*** <u>***thunders***</u> ***. . .*** (*Hebrews 12:25–26*
says that God's voice then <u>shook</u> the earth as of an
earth quake) . . . ***and lightnings, and the voice of the
trumpet exceeding loud; so that all the people in
the camp trembled.*** This was all done as an example of things to come. ***Hebrews 12:18–29*** explains
that Mt. Sinai represented darkness and blackness,
and one that was defiled with human hands (by our
own works . . . that could be <u>touched</u>), of the which
was consumed by the fire of God's word when He
came down with great power and glory by Mt. Zion.
***Hebrews 12:1 Seeing we also are compassed about
with so great a*** <u>***cloud***</u> ***of witnesses . . .*** Hmmm. Isn't
Jesus coming in the cloud? His witnesses? Of which
He will surely rain down the fire of His word upon
Esau, that Mt. Sinai. Get ready folks! (Which is also
what will happen at the end of the world, because
this Mt. Sinai, the world, is the worldly Jerusalem,
but when the heavenly Jerusalem rains down hail-
stones and coals of fire, this world will be consumed
in literal fire). Look in ***Hebrews 12:16–17.*** Do you
think that there is a reason that the writer of Hebrews
mentions Esau right before he speaks of the con-
sumption? Because Esau will be as Ishmael, even
as Sodom and Gomorrah. And why did he call Esau
a fornicator? Isn't it because he has cheated on his
wife? He is the seed of the adulterer and whore, as

Babylon. Babylon has drunk of the <u>wine</u> of the wrath of God, that wicked doctrine, so that they can't see straight or walk straight. And who was it that drank this wine? (***Isaiah 28:7*** will tell you. Folks, please bother to read these verses, <u>PLEASE</u>!!) They have cheated on God, their husband, and become one with the world, born of sin. ***James 4:4 Ye adulterers and adulteresses! Know ye not that the friendship with the world is enmity against God?*** They love the glory of the world, its power, money, praise of men and lusts of the flesh, like fornication and adultery.

And again in ***John 12*** when Jesus returned to Jerusalem He said ***"Father, glorify thy name." There came a voice from heaven saying, "I have both glorified it, and will glorify it <u>again</u>." 12:29 The people therefore that stood by and heard said that it <u>thundered</u>, others said an angel spoke to him.*** But later on, in ***12:34,*** (though the people had just got through lauding and praising Jesus in ***12:13*** because they saw that He had come, they knew who He was), they asked in ***12:34*** even after the angel spoke to him, ***"Who is this Son of Man?"*** Wasn't it because their understanding was darkened by Satan? So that, even though they saw Him, and knew Him, and praised God that He was come, the next moment they did not know Him. So Jesus says in ***12:35 Yet a*** *little while is the light with you, <u>walk</u> while ye have the light, lest darkness come upon you, for He that walks in darkness knows not where he is going.* And in *12:39–40* it says that the reason they didn't believe was because Satan hardened their heart. And again in *12:36* it says, *Jesus did hide himself from them.* Isn't Jesus the Word of God? So indeed only a little while the light was with us, because these events happened as an example, foretelling us of what was to come spiritually. Look around *John 9:4,* Jesus said *I must work the works of Him that sent me, while it is day, the night comes when no man can work.* The covenant that I am and will be writing to you is the Word of God, Rebecca . . . that new wine, which puts a new song in our hearts, our Joy. At least to those who have their names written in God's book of life . . . that is, his memory. Jesus said at the supper table before He was betrayed that he wouldn't drink of the <u>wine</u> of God again until He drank it <u>new</u> with us at the coming of His Kingdom. Am I at all telling anyone to do anything against Christ? Am I myself now doing anything against Him? What is my motive? To take over your church? Money? Glory from humans? Jesus said, *If any man will <u>do</u> His will, He shall know of the doctrine, whether I speak of myself or of God.* Don't let *John 12:42–43* happen. Don't be afraid to confess the truth. *1 John 4:2 Whosoever believes that Jesus Christ is come in the flesh,* in <u>us</u>, *is of God. 1 John 2:7 Brethren, I write no new commandment unto you but an old commandment which you had from the beginning,* (the word), *2:8*

Again, a <u>new</u> commandment, (word), *I write to you, because the darkness is past, and the true light now shines.* Didn't Jesus say that if we would believe, then we would see the glory of God? This is the glory of God for those who have believed.

This church I hope by now is not ashamed and does believe Jesus. I have left ya'll to preach this gospel to your own as I know you have already begun to do. I would do an injustice if I did not give you the opportunity to give birth yourselves. *2 Corinthians 5:12 I give you an occasion to glory on my behalf.* If anyone believes this gospel, use this book to teach with, *2 Corinthians 4:13 I believed, therefore I have spoken.* (The dead don't speak, only the living, so this scripture is also saying that eternal life comes through faith). I guarantee you all hell, the waters of the deep, are about to split wide open as the staff of Moses did to the Red Sea, and the wheat will be divided from the chaff. All I ask is that no one person *glory in another man's labor made ready to our hand (2 Corinthians 10:16)* but just to say you have received this doctrine of which you also want to embrace and implement in this church. If this is done, I suspect that you will receive and embrace the very Word of God in more ways than you thought. This is truly *the way, the truth, and life.* And I will stand with you (you can say my name too), and continue to speak through e-mail. I will <u>show</u> my face there if you want also, though I will not <u>speak</u> face to face. I don't go away because I am ashamed, nor because I fear, but for you. I'm not saying that at first you won't be put to shame if you do this, but the Lord will revive you; He did me. Hmmm. I wonder what the Catholic Church would think of all this. Think I will pay them a visit if you don't need me. I am ready to run. I will definitely still write you all though. There is much still left to say and your strength is my strength. Again, if I need you, *I give you an occasion to glory on my behalf.* If I could raise the dead I would, (though I have). If I could give sight to the blind I would, (though I have). If I could cast out devils I would, (though I have), or heal people of their sickness, or make the deaf to hear, I would do all these things. But I wonder that even if this was done if anyone who still may have doubts would believe. I plan on continuing where I left off in the book of Romans a good while back now on the next letter. *"Peace be unto you."*

===========

I really don't know what to say now. I said that I would start in Romans, but considering who is now getting my e-mails I feel like it would be insulting! Ha! Trust me, I know that these things have been taught a lot and that you all know them. I hope I don't bore you. But I will speak as if to someone who has never read this because truly I am putting together a book to pass out to churches and people that don't hear the radio. I am soooo happy that I have brothers!

Don't think I can say, "You have no idea!" OOOps, and sisters? I like being able to go through this stuff because it seems like when I start thinking about it, stuff just starts popping in my head. Never know what is there!! I am so excited I can hardly contain myself at times! I tell you no lie, <u>much</u> of the stuff that I write I learn as I go. I can read the bible again and again and understand or learn <u>nowhere near</u> as much as I do when I try to write and share. This tells me something that I am absolutely convinced of: the more I share, the more I am increased. The more <u>glory</u> that I give to you to give, the more I get. If not in this life, then in heaven. Truly there is a God. I know that God will reward all accordingly, even in this life. If anyone should be content with what they have from God it should be me, but still there is this stupidity rising up within me trying to take, take, take. It takes away joy when I try and compare what I have with other people. That is actually stupid. When I focus only on what I have been given, irregardless of anyone else, then truly I am thankful and content. And the Lord multiplies it when I give it away. I love myself so much that I have given to you all to give. Use me! Use me!!

I want to try and express something, not that it is not known already, but just because I want to say it. And that is this: I cannot help who I am. And I cannot help what I am doing. It is not my fault that God is doing what He is doing in me or that he has chosen me to do it through. And it is <u>not</u> me doing anything. Jealousy among us is dumb. I would love to take credit or to have you all think I am skilled, that I purposely plan these things out, but I am telling you that I don't even mean to do or say a lot of the stuff I do. I can do no more <u>or less</u> than what is appointed for me. He has a mind of His own and I cannot fight Him. His Love has taken me captive. When I fight, (and believe me I have), I lose worse, because then I <u>see myself</u> how I truly am. No sooner than I say, "Oh, I would never sin in <u>that</u> way," I have done that very thing. I call it getting <u>slammed</u>. And I have been slammed so many times in different ways that I just go ahead and slam myself, why not? I just don't even care anymore. And I slam, (humble), myself not because <u>I myself</u> do it, but because it is through being humbled so much through experiences that the Lord has manifested himself in me. So when I slam myself it is not me, but Him. But I don't understand, <u>know</u> that it is Him unless I exalt myself so many times. And the more I exalt myself the more humble I end up, because I have done it so many times that I know I would if He didn't stop me. And because by the time I finally figure it out that I would, then I have done it so much, which tells me that it is not me that understands, but it is Him who understands. The moment I think that I understand the truth, then it is taken from me, so that when it is given to me I understand that it is Him. And since it is Him that understands that it is Him, I don't understand this. If I do, then I don't, because it is Him. Ha! You can definitely say I am possessed. I have to say that I definitely don't mind! And that's the thing, I don't mind . . . because I am possessed! Unfortunately/fortunately, you all were around when I was talking. You have been given the same Spirit. Believe me, you will fight, and you will lose. But don't worry about <u>anything</u>. Everything is in His hand, even when you take it back. ***Hebrews 10:39 We are not of them that fall back unto perdition, but of them that believe to the saving of the soul.*** Because when you fall back you will be so tortured mentally until you do what you're supposed to, that you will. Suggestion: don't say you won't fall. And don't say that at times you won't believe the truth . . . trust me, you won't. (So that you may know that it is Him that believes, that you may <u>know</u> Him.) All I have to do is sincerely try and do what I am supposed to (with <u>diligence</u>, but not worry), and everything will be okay. And I know that you all will try, because you have what I do. Just say, "Here Lord, I give everything to you, this ministry, everything. Will you take care of it for me? I can't." And He will. We'll do fine. I really do love you all. Peace. Darrell

Again, I know that you all know some of these things and that your eyes have been opened, but bear with the simple stuff because mixed in you might find something else. And it never hurts to review. I just go with what I am led to, but my base camp will be the book of Romans. I really want to get to some serious stuff, but we got time.

I would like to say that there are commandments given by the Apostle Paul that are extremely important to keep. Let's not argue with believers over anything at all. If there are disagreements, why not just let it lay and pray about it? Time will tell <u>us</u> where we are wrong if we ask God for truth and walk in love. This is the Lord's day, no more another's. I think that when we "give up," a lot of times people just come to the truth themselves, if they at all read the New Testament, and more importantly are <u>obedient</u> to Jesus. A lot of times when I try too hard it just has a reverse effect. Do not argue. Then you're both disobedient. If there are stressful discussions just leave it alone. I think that I should also add that it is not smart to hang out with a person who is constantly speaking against the truth or trying to draw you away from doing right. ***Colossians 4:5 Walk in wisdom toward them that are without.*** Satan is really going to be attacking those who are believers now. Let me say it again, watch out! ***Romans 2:28 For he is not a Jew which is one outwardly,*** in appearance, or actually meaning <u>naturally born</u> of Abraham. ***2:29 but he is a Jew which is one inwardly, in the spirit, <u>whose praise is not of men,</u>*** (humans), ***but of God.*** As I said before, the Jews were the physical example of the spiritual Jews that were to come . . . Christians. The true Jews are Abrahams seed through the faith he had. The Jews of that time relied too heavily on the fact that they were the descendants of Abraham, in particular the leaders, and that just because of this God would give them the promised land, regardless of their actions. So John the Baptist, who preached the same gospel, warned them before Christ came in *Matthew 3:8 Bring forth therefore fruits meet for repentance, and think not to say within yourselves, "We have Abraham as our father." For God is able of these stones to raise up children to Abraham.* Indeed, because some of them didn't listen He denied them as His children and said that Gentiles were His instead, whom He also called the <u>stones</u> of his temple: *1 Peter 2:5 ye also, as lively stones, are built up a spiritual house* for God to live in. Jesus prophesied, speaking of the stones of the temple in *Luke 22:6 the days will come in the which there shall not be left one stone upon another that shall not be thrown down.* Again John the Baptist speaks in *Matthew 3:7* asking them: *who has warned you to flee from the wrath to come?* What was the wrath? Christ's coming. Because there are two kinds of <u>sword</u>, or wrath. Look in *3:10 And <u>now</u> also the axe,* the word of God, *is laid unto the root,* the inner part or life, *of the trees.* OOOh! Look . . . treeee! (Which is us). The axe will test the tree and see what kind it is. *Every tree which brings not forth good fruit is hewn down,* removed from its place, and refined in fire so that when the actual coming happens they may be acceptable to God. Trees grow in the wilderness on different mountains and hills. Some mountains are high and mighty as with the trees, and then there are the humble low places and valleys. Some trees are

Darrell Gilbert

66

green because they have life in themselves, whose glory, or <u>leaf</u> withers not, as the first Psalm says and <u>clap their hands</u> with joy in God as says Isaiah. And there are some trees that are dead, depending on if they are watered and nourished right, and depending on what season they are born in. Because again, giving prophecy of a time of darkness which would also start in their generation, on his way to be <u>crucified</u>, Jesus said in *Luke 23:28 and 31 Daughters of Jerusalem weep not for me, but weep for yourselves and for your children, for if they do these things in a green tree,* during His time, *what shall be done in the dry?* In a time when there would be no water. John said that <u>now</u>, that is, during his time the axe is laid unto the trees. Turn to *Psalms 74:5,* it says: *A man was famous according as he had lifted up axes upon the thick,* (the proud), *trees.* Who do you think that man was? Please read this Psalm now, remembering that the Lord has purchased us with His own blood according to Paul.

———————

If we will at all <u>try</u>, with a sincere and pure heart, to do <u>all</u> God asks, then I think you may be surprised at how quickly the Lord is ready to help and forgive. Just at least <u>stay open-minded</u> to these things.

The same passages written in Matthew about what John said, who preached the ways of Jesus

Christ right before He came, who was also beheaded by the government, are written in the book of *Luke 3.* Many people that heard John were convicted and asked what they should do, including soldiers. Now as we know, soldiers meant those who were in the army, right? John commanded in *3:14 Do violence to no man.* Now I am certain that if they kept this command, they were in trouble. Are we justified by the works of the law, as the children of Israel conquered nations? Again Paul says in *2 Timothy 2:4 No man that wars* spiritually *entangles himself with the affairs of this life, that he may please Him who has chosen him to be a soldier.* Because He says again in *2 Corinthians: the weapons of our warfare are not carnal.* As a Christian then we should not be caught up in the political environment, but should let the world run the world. The Lord has appointed the kings of the world to run it; our job is just to make the truth known, by action and word. Again Paul says in *1 Thessalonians 5:15 See that none render evil for evil unto any man, but always follow that which is good, both among yourselves,* among brethren, *and to all.* Some things may seem a bit radical that I say, but Jesus wasn't exactly normal. *Luke 9:24 For whosoever will save his life shall lose it, and whosoever will lose his life for my sake will save it.* What does He mean by life? He answers in the next verse: *For what is a man advantaged if he gain the whole world and lose himself?* So then your life means this world and the things of it: possessions, position, reputation, friends and family, freedom, and maybe literally. It is when we lose our life, <u>die</u>, that we gain an <u>inward life</u> ... yourself. Because just as when we die literally we will be in the presence of God, when we are willing to give up this life we move into the presence of God. It is the way the Spirit manifests Himself in us, through suffering, death. When we decide to live in holiness, <u>strict</u> obedience, this will happen. So we should not look at trouble as something bad, but embrace it as an opportunity; the Lord has opened a door for us to know Him. He is saying, "Come up here." *1 John 2:15 Love not the world, neither the things in the world. If any man love the world, the love of the Father is not in him.* Our focus then should not be on this life, but that which is to come, and our actions show our focus. Jesus said in *Luke 9:23 If any will come after me, let him deny himself,* his own wants, *and take up his cross,* which is what God's will is for you, *and follow me.* Again Jesus gives His opinion concerning possession and even family when asked in *Luke 9:57* when different people wanted to be with Him. To the one He said he might not have a place to lay his head here in this world. To another who was compassionate and caring, being thoughtful of his own father who had just died, Christ said: *Follow me and let the dead bury their dead.* So then we should let the world, those who are dead inwardly, be concerned with the world. But those who are alive in Christ should have their mind on the eternal. And this was the man's own father! The next verse was a rebuke to the one that said, *Lord, I will follow thee, but first let me go home and say good-bye to them at home.* Are relationships in this world eternal? Or are your relationships eternal in Christ? Example: You own a business. There is a contract brewing worth over $20,000. But in order to get the contract you must lie. What would you do? Would you say, well, I have family at home, that would be abusive and I would neglect my kids. I have a responsibility. You sure do. Do you trust that God will take care of how your kids turn out, or do you think that you can raise them better? Do you believe in Jesus, or yourself and your own way of thinking? One child gets disciplined harshly and reacts in rebellion, citing abuse and neglect. Another is subjected to the same and turns out with strong character. Who is it that molds what is within? Maybe you're single and looking for a wife. First Paul says in *1 Corinthians 7:27 Are you free from a wife? Seek not a wife.* But if so, are you anxious or worried? Is your mind consumed with the opposite sex, your job . . . or God? Do you exclude other guys or girls from going out with you because of jealousy or fear they may possibly keep you from your worldly hope? If so, you love the world too much. This is a lack of faith, because if you really trusted in God, then you would rest in the assurance that if that person is the one for you, then it will happen regardless of whether someone else may be a bit better looking. And if God wants to give you a better job, then it doesn't matter if someone else may or may not be better qualified or bid lower. John the Baptist said also to the centurion in *Luke 3:14 Be content with your wages.* And if they are not the one, then you are stressing yourself for nothing. Trust that God knows better, because if you do get the wrong one, I guarantee you that you will be miserable. Jesus, in my favorite chapter and parable of the bible, says in *Luke 14:20* when talking about those whom God is calling to Himself, says one answered, ***I have married a wife, and therefore I cannot come.*** Maybe He put that person there who got what you wanted, to keep you from misery. Jesus said, ***Matthew 6:25 Therefore I say unto you, take no thought for your life,*** because it is in denying this world that you confess your hope in another. I know this, if you give the job to another, or the mate to another, then God sees it. Do it in Jesus' name and say, "Lord, you know what I really want, and I trust in you that you know better than me what I want, please give me my wants as I have done so to them. Please help me, and keep me." Then see what happens. Be patient though and desire <u>spiritual</u> things. Because when you do such things you are really seeking after God and knocking on heaven's door. The Lord said in *Luke 6:37–38 **Give, and it shall be given to you. Forgive, and you shall be forgiven. 11:9–13 Knock and it shall be opened unto you. Ask, and it shall be given,*** that is. . the Holy Ghost as *11:13* says. ***Seek, and you will find.*** The <u>Lord</u> wants to be your spouse, the <u>Lord</u> wants to be your Father, and He wants to give you <u>His</u> riches. And though in past times you may have seen others give themselves to God and end up spiritually desolate, I invite you to say, "I know now why Lord, I believe your Word,

Re-bek'ah

71

that this is the true God. I want to trust in <u>you</u> now. Please show me how, please don't let me down, I am sorry for all I have done. Take my life, all that I am, let me not take it back ever again, but commit me <u>wholly</u> to you, make me into what you want me to be." In Jesus' name.

The word <u>sober</u> is the key. It means: quiet, not loud or unnecessary, not excessive or exaggerated, restrained, temperate, modest, chaste. The Lord is a God of peace. There is nothing in creation wicked in and of itself, but in the way we abuse what God has given: Food or chocolate cake is not wicked, but eating too much is. Alcohol is not wrong, but getting drunk is. Drugs are not wrong, but the manipulation and abuse of them are. Money is not evil, but the love of it is. Sex is not wrong, but having it with everyone and their momma is . . . it should be restrained to marriage and done in love. Get the idea? Speaking is not wrong, but being a blabbermouth is, and using unnecessary words are. Strict honesty is a must. The Lord said, *Every idle word that men shall speak, they will have to give account for at the day of judgment.* Music and instruments are not evil, but being loud and unrestrained is. Wearing clothes is definitely not wrong, but wearing expensive suits, *gold, pearls and costly array* as Paul the Apostle puts it, and Peter too, is. Better to wear blue jeans and a tee-shirt. Exercising is definitely not wrong, but inflating yourselves in pride is not wise. Playing games or sports is not wicked, but violence and the uncontrolled desire to dominate is, *Galatians 5:26 Let us not be desirous of glory, envying one another, pro-voking one another* to anger. So then humility, which is the opposite of pride, is what we seek for, because Satan's fall was His pride. He thought that He was something that He wasn't. And any person who is in authority over the church, if they think that they are greater than Paul the Apostle, that <u>all</u> these things shouldn't be done, is a fool. Nor did the Apostles have life insurance. It is good for a person to go to work. Jesus said in *John 13:16 The servant is not greater than His master.* And, *John 18:36 My kingdom is not of this world.* More about what pleases God is found in: *Romans 12, Galatians 5:19–26, Ephesians 4:17-end, & Colossians ch. 3–4*

———————

Romans 3:1 What advantage then has the Jew? Or what profit is there of circumcision? Circumcision was a commandment given to Abraham to do to all his <u>seed</u>, or children, which are called Jews. It is the cutting off of the foreskin. In the early church there were a lot of Jews who insisted that Christians must be circumcised, probably because it was preached of Paul that we were justified in God's eyes through the covenant made with Abraham, which was before the Law of Moses. But Paul taught that circumcision was not meant to be taken literally. Look at *4:11 And he,* Abraham, *received the <u>sign</u> of circumcision, a <u>seal</u>*

of the righteousness of the faith. So just as literally all Jews, the people of God, show in their hidden parts by the cutting off of the covering of their sin that they are God's from birth, *(Job 31:33)* in the same way when we are born spiritually we are <u>sealed</u> by the Holy Ghost as one of God's permanently when we keep the law of circumcision. That is, when we cut off the flesh, taking away the covering and admitting that we have sinned, (particularly after the last day). *Colossians 2:11 ye are circumcised with the circumcision made without hands, in putting off the body of the sins of the flesh.* Anyway, when Christ came and gave a new law, (or rather a <u>covenant</u> that was older than Moses' law, but wasn't <u>made known</u> until he fulfilled it), it pretty much became worthless for a Jew to be a Jew, or for them to continue in the covenant of Moses, keeping the laws of Moses literally. So Paul asks in *Romans 3:1 What advantage then has the Jew? 3:3 for what if some did not believe? 3:2* explains that they were lucky in that they had the advantage of having a pattern of the spirit world through the book of the law, and so could more easily believe in Christ because it pointed to Him. And originally and firstly God came to them through revelations made by the prophets. But if they still denied that <u>Jesus died and rose again,</u> and continued in the covenant of Moses, keeping its laws faithfully, did they still have an advantage? Could they still be considered righteous before God by their works? Paul answers the question with another question: *3:3 Shall their unbelief make the faith,* the covenant, *of God without effect?* Because if God continued to say that they were righteous even though they denied Christ then He also would be denying His own Word, giving Jesus' resurrection no power, (or effect), to save. He also would then be making Himself a liar because He <u>swore</u> that he would perform this oath to Abraham. God is not going to become unjust, or lie, (because He can't), so that they may be righteous just because they are Jews, or because they have been circumcised. *3:4 Let God be true but every man a liar.* (Just in case you haven't gotten it yet, these same things apply to us now.) When you say that you have lied, or turned against God, you say the truth and thereby justify yourself, because the scriptures foretold that all will have sinned. And Christ wouldn't have needed to come if they weren't in sin. I would like to also mention here that when we believed in Jesus we became Jews and were circumcised. If we then deny Him through our actions as explained before, we make ourselves liars. <u>If you aren't in faith you are under the law</u>. And if you are under a law you are in sin because sin is the disobedience of the law, (and no one is perfect). There is a fine line folks that probably varies with each person and that only God knows as to whether you step over. He does what He wants. It would be healthy for you to do as much good as you can, and try as hard as you can, that *you may find grace to help in time of need (Hebrews 4:16).*

    Romans 2:25 For circumcision verily profits if thou keep the law, but if thou be a breaker of

the law, thy circumcision is made uncircumcision.
Typically when the covenant of Jesus came to fruition, as it also has now, those who kept the ways of
God saw the truth because they had it in them. But
those who were disobedient denied Jesus. This they
did for themselves and everyone else, so that we
could <u>know</u> Him when they rejected and crucified
Him (which is the reason in the first place that God
allowed some of His people to turn from Him). ***3:5
But if our unrighteousness commend the righteousness of God, what shall we say? Is God unrighteous
who takes vengeance?*** If the Jews fulfilled the law in
condemning Jesus, shouldn't they be justified because
they proved by their evil deeds that God's Word is
true, making Him righteous? And ***3:7 If the truth of
God has more abounded through my lie,*** my denial
of Christ, ***unto His glory,*** because now we can all
become one with God, ***why am I judged as a sinner?
3:8 and not rather say, "Let us do evil, that good
may come?"*** Also as explained with Lazarus, God
does allow some to fall away to fulfill the scriptures,
that He might <u>make Himself known</u>; His personality, kindness, love etc. And so mercy may abound
through them along with all other fruits, especially
when they are resurrected by Him. But if they don't
repent, Paul still justifies God: ***3:8 whose damnation is right,*** and in ***3:5 I speak as a man.*** Because
only human thinking and a fool says God is wrong or
thinks they are better than anyone else just because
they are a <u>Jew</u>. There is much more to say on this
subject but I better send something. Peace, Darrell

I know that some of this stuff is so simple that it makes you want to barf, but believe me, there is something behind it all that has to do with the mystery of God, (the questions you want me to answer), that I am building up too, okay? I know that if I just blurt something out you aren't going to believe it, but if I give scripture as a pattern then you will . . . hopefully. These things might be helpful in getting others to believe also. This is an addition to the last letters' subject found in *Galatians 3:15–22.* Might as well be thorough. Remember one thing: *Sin is the transgression of the law.* So the law, <u>any law</u> if you are under it, is damnation. If you have not read what I have written before on the book of Galatians, it would be extremely helpful, that way you will not think I am wicked. I appreciate it. Also, please do not think that I am trying to put anyone at this church in particular down who have repented. Actually I never try to put people down, but I am just speaking the word. I understand that some of this stuff can be taken offensively if a person is proud.

Galatians 3:15 Brethren, I speak after the manner of men . . . simply. *Though but a man's covenant,* that is, God made it with us mere mortals, *yet confirmed,* by an oath. *No man disannuls or adds to it.* So how do we disannul it? Through putting ourselves under the law, because the Law of Moses, (which was an example of the wrath to come), was <u>after</u> the covenant with Abraham: *3:17 **The covenant that was confirmed before of God in Christ, the law, which was** (added) **430 years after, cannot <u>disannul,</u>** (or <u>cancel out</u> the new law, or Truth), **that it should make the promise of <u>no effect</u> (Romans 3:3).** So because the covenant <u>cannot</u> be disannulled and God cannot lie, if you revert back to the law, (your old works), you disannul yourself to the covenant of faith and it becomes of no effect, without power; you make <u>yourself</u> a liar, not God. **Galatians 5:4 Christ is <u>become</u> of no effect unto you,** (as if before now Christ <u>was</u> effective), **whosoever of you are justified,** perfected, **by the law,** (sin), **ye are <u>fallen from grace.</u>** (Try to tell them that). So the curse had already started happening at the time of Paul because of "Jews" teaching false doctrines and their own ways, being carried away with their own culture and justifying themselves. They tried to add beliefs out of the law that were anti-Christ, canceling out what they didn't want to hear and leading people to damnation. But Paul, who was a strict Jew and a murderer before conversion, constantly battled his own culture, the law. **3:19 Why then the law? It was <u>added</u> because of transgressions till the seed should come,** (Jesus alone), **to whom the promise was made.** And just as then the law was added after the real covenant, so after Christ came then came damnation through His law because of their disobedience, until the covenant came to maturity again and we have the real Christ resurrected <u>within us:</u> **Galatians 3:16 Now to Abraham and his seed were** *the promises made. He said not "And to seeds," as of many, but as of one.* Paul says this to let them (he is speaking to Christians) know that if they received another Spirit besides Jesus after believing then they were not a child of the promise. If there is an Esau or an Ishmael in us we are no more of promise: *3:18 For if the inheritance be of the law, it is <u>no more</u> of promise.* And the scriptures show here that they had begun to do so. And according to the faith of Christ, that covenant, as I have numerous times proved without a reasonable doubt, it foretold that we would fall away and that Son of perdition would murder Jesus. *Galatians 1:6 I marvel that you are so soon removed from Him to another gospel.* Can a Christian be <u>removed</u>? *1:7 which is not another, but there be some that would pervert the word of Christ. 1:10 For do I seek to please men?* So even though we disannulled it through transgression, in our disannulment, we proved it right and so didn't disannul it. So *3:21* says *is the law against the promises of God? God Forbid!* The law fulfilled itself in condemning us and to those who were obedient kept us until Christ came. *For if there had been a law given which could have given life, verily righteousness should have been by the law.* And Jesus' covenant did perfect some, (and to those who were obedient kept us to fruition). *3:22 But the scripture has concluded all under sin,* because of the death of Christ on the cross and Judas. *3:24 So then the law was our schoolmaster to bring us to Christ, that we might be justified by faith.* Preaching that Jesus died and

Re-bek'ah

79

rose again is not wrong, but believing only that is not enough anymore because of Rebecca. Is there any new law given under Rebecca?

———————————————

Okay, I have just re-read some of what I have wrote in the last letter and can see that it can seem quite confusing and contradictory. I just happen to believe that the scriptures say more than just one thing at a time, and there are many truths that are hidden. I have to laugh at myself, I <u>know</u> that there are some who are going to misunderstand what I was trying to say. I better try and use softer words and quit calling people a fool before I embarrass myself. I only use words like fool because I am a King James Version brainwashed dude. To keep things simple I will try to just speak of the things as it is written. *Galatians 3:15 -22* simply says that you can't be perfected under the Law of Moses; that the covenant of Moses was added after the real one and the seed is not literal or many, but one, Christ; that if you stick to the Law of Moses once the covenant of Christ is here then not only will it not perfect you, but you are no more considered a child of promise because you deny Christ; that the law was given to keep us until the seed came and so originally was not against Christ. Simple enough? Trust me though, consider what I said in the last letter. Didn't the Lord create darkness and light by His word? Which one existed first? I want to officially apologize because <u>I am wrong</u> for calling anyone a fool. See, I have made an idiot of myself. I know that there are some that have said, "No man can disannul or add to the covenant, so Rebecca cannot be true." Better have the faith that Abraham did literally then and attempt to kill our children if no one adds to the original covenant. Hope you're circumcised literally too. Are Christians cursed? Better revert back to the Law of Moses, because Paul also in ***Galatians 3:10*** quoted from the Old Testament, ***"Cursed is everyone that contiueth not in all things that are written in the book of the law to do them."*** But just as then if you didn't confess the resurrection of Christ you disannulled the covenant, even so now you have disannulled the covenant of Abraham if you don't confess the resurrection of Christ. And if you confess this resurrection, you say the others have led to the death of Christ in us, as those covenants also did. God, foretelling in both the Law of Moses and in the Covenant of Jesus that we would turn against Him, has before provided a plan of salvation through the blood of His only Son Jesus Christ: His resurrection.

Sometimes I think that going through this stuff may be bad because it brings up arguments. But supposedly it is profitable to study according to it. I don't mean to offend. I think as I said before that there are more things said in scripture than what meets the eye. Yes, you are saved solely by faith. That's the bottom line, right? That there is nothing that you can do that can earn salvation. But I do believe that God is a rewarder of good once you're saved. Nothing wrong with that, right? I think I should tell you a bit about myself. I have only recently, in the past year or so started going to church, though I have been a Christian much longer. I have never read Martin Luther, John Calvin, or any other commentary <u>whatsoever</u>. I have never studied any other version of the bible besides the King James except only very, very, little of the New King James version. A big reason for this is that at least half or about half of the time that I have been a Christian has been spent in prison, where I had little access to radio, books, etc. because most of that time was spent in lock down or solitary confinement in one way or another. I will say that I have had persecution for my beliefs, which are quite strict. And that I spent a lot more time in prison than I should have for this reason. I don't like to say stuff like that because I don't care to glory. Even when or if I did have access to fellowship with other Christians, I chose not to do so. I have had many, <u>many</u>, powerful, unbelievable spiritual experiences to the point that I went "crazy." I will admit it. I became ridiculously obedient to the point that I wouldn't even move from a respectful body position, if you can only try to understand why. I was scared to death. I was sent in prison to several psychiatrists who indeed marveled at my answers. I saw the faces of others when their chins literally dropped with eyes wide open. Such things assured me that I wasn't crazy or seeing things. They tried to give me drugs to calm my mind in jail. I was openly humiliated in so many ways

that I really don't care to go into all. But for one, for
many years everyone thought and looked on me as a
homosexual, even flirting with me because they had
to put me on safekeeping status, where all the drag
queens were. They wanted to protect me because
they thought I was crazy. Kind of funny. Boy I could
tell you some stories! But see, I don't care what anyone thinks when it comes down to it. Call me a fool;
it's nothing new. Throw me in prison or beat me up,
or spit in my face for Jesus; believe me, it is nothing
new. The guards at prison tried to cripple me, literally, and several of them while I was on the ground
kicked me in the ribs and beat on me, then wrote me
a case and sent me to lock up <u>for assaulting them</u>. All
because I wouldn't expose myself in a really graphic
way to several homosexuals and females standing
by, because I thought it was immoral. They of course
thought I was just too embarrassed, and wondered
that if I was right then why I was the only Christian
to refuse to obey their orders. Of course, it is quite
embarrassing to do such a thing, but I wouldn't lose
my life over it. It was my convictions that did that.
And even if I was wrong as they claimed for disobeying authority, I <u>know</u> that God knows my heart and
intentions, and He honored my sincerity, especially
when others didn't. Sometimes I take for granted that
every Christian is strong, that just because they get
called a bad name (poor thing), doesn't mean they
should be offended. And yes, I say this and as soon
as I do I know someone will call me a fool and I am
the one who will get mad. I think that the most tortur-

ing test that God put me through though, and there are many, are the years I spent without His presence. I was extremely faithful, but He left me. Of course, you probably wouldn't believe that. That's a whole other story.

Anyway, I will indeed go through the scriptures here. Please try and keep an open mind. (But if it is evil, do indeed close your mind.) Darrell

Epilogue

The following detailed explanation is what I have written to believers who have responded to this book at the e-mail address located on the back of the last page. From these discussions I have come to the conclusion that few, if any, who have read the book have understood what the salvation of Re-bek'ah is. I have found it very hard to explain and prove. I really want you to know before going on to the rest of the book what this point is. I would be very thankful for your sincere questions or positive comments.

It is very important throughout this entire book, you don't look at the stories told in a literal sense (with a "carnal," or "fleshly" mind), but in a spiritual sense. Before making my main point, I tried to exercise the brain (in particularly in pages 17–19) with many of those stories of the Bible that Paul explains spiritually to show that this is truly the way that the original elect saw the scriptures. You can look at those pages again now. It is the way that the gospel was preached to that generation of believers, if they believed. And it is the way that the truth was "hidden." Please remember the things that I am saying here: Faith in the resurrection of His Son from the dead, and in His promise of life has always been the way that God has justified His people. It is the same faith, but it is revealed and fulfilled in different ways. There is truly only one sacrifice for our sins, and only one covenant, one salvation, just as there is only "one" God. (Page 50.)

Another very important point in pages 12–16, which pages 20 through 25 expound on, is the fact that no doubt everything was planned out from "the beginning" with God—predestination. That there is a literal pattern of what is happening spiritually given in the stories of the Bible, especially of the children of Israel being delivered by the hand of Moses. This order of events cannot be broken; it is the Word of God and He can't lie. So if you deny the story then you make yourself a liar. Yea, indeed He did deliver the Jews literally originally through Moses and the law. The generation of Moses, and the events that took place literally then, were a completion of God's promise to Abraham. They were the end of the story. But the scriptures explain that it was the beginning of the spiritual story that was fulfilled spiritually in Paul's time through Christ. (Bottom of page 13.)

This paragraph will go with what I wrote in pages 26 and half of 27. That spiritual fulfillment of the story of Moses is Sarah and Isaac spiritually, because it is the Word of God. The spiritual interpretation of the story of Moses is part of the gospel of Christ. That generation of people, Isaac, were born spiritually through belief in the literal death and resurrection story of Christ. The death and resurrection story is Sarah. The result of the story through faith is an Isaac. Isaac is not a "fleshly" or physical Isaac, but a spiritual Isaac. Just as Sarah is not a physical or literal Sarah. Isaac is not one person, but many persons in one body who were born spiritually to Sarah the covenant of Jesus. More of that gospel Word, for example, is this spiritual interpretation of the scriptures: [Paul explains that] Abraham had a firstborn son who was wicked, Ishmael. Paul claims that the people who were under the literal covenant of Moses became spiritually once Christ came to power. That is, when Isaac was born. He claims that all who are under the law of Moses have then become wicked, "born" of Hagar the bondwoman. Hagar is the covenant of Moses literally. Ishmael is the result of that covenant. "Isaac" though, who Paul claims to be so to speak, was born to Sarah, which was the Covenant and Word of Jesus Christ.

Let's look at this story of Moses carefully and now we will get into Rebecca/Jacob, which, in a way is the same covenant . . . though a bit different. Consider that Paul, claiming that their generation was the beginning of the spiritual story of Moses (how that they were delivered spiritually out into the wilderness through Christ . . . which story is Sarah resulting in Isaac), in the book of Thessalonians foretold that there was to be a spiritual "fall" that was to come. A "falling away." (See page 42, very important.) The writer of Hebrews speaks here as he also warned on pages 14 and 15 of the same fall repeatedly and explains how the children of Israel "fell" in the wilderness after they were delivered by Moses. This shows us then where we are in the order of events. The writer of Hebrews and Thessalonians knew that generation was the beginning of the spiritual fulfillment of the deliverance of the Jews from Egypt into the wilderness as I explained. And just as the children rebelled and fell in the wilderness, even so it would happen spiritually. And after the fall there would be another seed of Abraham, Jacob, raised up through the story of Christ spiritually in the same way that God delivered the Jews through Joshua. This is that generation of Jacob's, that day of salvation, the time of Joshua. Soooo . . .

The salvation of Rebecca then is on page 41 starting mainly with the sentence: Galatians 3:22 the scripture has judged all under sin, because the death of Christ on the cross foretold what would happen spiritually within us. So then the story of Christ has been completed spiritually since the literal death and resurrection. That the Jesus given by that literal gospel of Christ would (as it foretold spiritually) become one with sin in us, in our heart, through our disobedience and be "crucified" by us the gentiles through "Judas." This is the wrath of God, the curse as I explained on pgs. 37–39 and claim at the very beginning of page 40 Christ has now delivered us from. So then Rebecca is the spiritual completion and fulfillment of the story of Jesus Christ. Jesus Christ has been resurrected spiritually. He is now risen again through belief of this Word, Rebecca: Jesus Christ has died and rose again. She is what we are born by through belief in it, and so therefore is our "mother," spiritually. Look at the end of page 41 at the scripture (John 17:22) where John calls Judas the Son of perdition. But in the beginning of page 42 Paul in Thessalonians says the son of perdition yet to be revealed was just now beginning to come. Now then, if they knew that Judas was the son of perdition and is dead, then how could they be foretelling of him literally? Judas then was the example of the spiritual "Judas." And not one person, but many in one body, an Esau. [2 Thess 2:3–12: Aren't our bodies the temple of God?] But it is prophesied also in those scriptures in Thessalonians, that Wicked would be shown, revealed by the Spirit of God and so "taken out of the way." This then is that revelation.

So then just as the generation of Moses and the people who were under his word became Ishmael when the spiritual Isaac came to be, even so now has the fleshly, false, literal Christ become Isaac's firstborn Esau because of Jacob coming to power. And as then, the end of the literal gospel of Moses was nothing more than a beginning to the real Word, even so now the end of the fleshly or false Christ has come (as Jesus says on page 42 "the things concerning me have an end"), because the real Christ has put him to death by His blood through His crucifixion and resurrection. Christ says He is the beginning and end. Whew!

Stay with me here. Who is it that reveals the wicked son? That consumes him by the Spirit and Word of His mouth by making him known as Paul says in 2 Thessalonians? Isn't it God through His Holy Ghost? So then let Him show you again the son of perdition out of the Old Testament. I hope you know the story of David. This is part of a letter that I wrote to my best friend and fellow Jacobi in prison: (Those who believe as we do are called Jacobean, or "Jacobi.")

I was reading in the book of 2 Samuel. I find it amazing how our gospel was foretold even back then. I never saw what I see in the stories until after I wrote Re-bek'ah. Strong assurance is given to me of the truth of it. You know that King David was the representation of that true King, Jesus Christ. And the things that happened to him foretold of events that have happened spiritually since. David had many servants, but he also made "sons." He established his kingdom above all. After his Kingdom was established there was one son, that son of perdition, Absalom, who rebelled against him, who was also hung on a tree (18:9–10). And there was no son of David that had the spiritual glory, dominion, power, and beauty that Absalom had, and he was perfect before God (14:25). He was a thief (15:6), desiring to be first, and betrayed the son of man with a kiss (15:5). Who with the kisses of his mouth (his words), flattered the people in the entrance to the city. He caused David and all his to be removed out of Jerusalem, to pass back "over the river" back into the "wilderness" (15:23). As he did David was "cursed" by a man from the family of the first King Saul (16:5–8, 19:21). Saul represented that first covenant's spiritual King of the Jews, given through Moses, who was removed and replaced by Christ. But then not only did David pass over that river, but Jordan also, all the way through the wilderness back to death (17:22). I think that it is important to note that the event happened after David established his Kingdom, because it further confirms that the events of Christ's crucifixion by the gentiles through Judas pointed to the spiritual fulfillment of those same events afterward, as the book of Revelation 19:10 says: The testimony of Jesus is the spirit of prophecy.

I will end with a brief explanation of a story in Joshua (I could go on and on). Remember on pages 73 and 74 how Paul explains true circumcision is the reception of the Holy Ghost. Look in the book of Joshua 5: 2–7. This will also further assure you of the truth of Rebecca. The people in the time of Paul were all circumcised spiritually as the people of the generation of Moses were literally. They all had the Ghost in full, to perfection. They were saints. Sons, not servants. (But only very few made it.) But it wasn't until Joshua led the children over Jordan in like manner as Moses over the Red Sea that the people were circumcised again (which is what is happening and about to happen through Rebecca). This is what I explain on p. 40–41. We have been in the wilderness, without the Spirit, since the time of the generation of Paul, but not wholly. Not as if the Lord has utterly forgotten us or that some would not be saved. It's just that no one has been perfected. But Jesus did say in John 8:35, "Verily, verily I say unto you, the servant abides not in the house forever, but the Son abides forever."

Dictionary

according: in harmony with; in agreement to; consistent with; as spoken; in accordance.

allegory: a symbolic representation of something else; something that symbolizes, represents, or holds another meaning.

begotten: created; to give life to; produce; living.

boast: to brag about; take pride in.

bondmaid: a female servant in bondage or slavery.

breach: an infraction of an obligation; a break; broken; a temporary gap.

commend: to give honor to; entrust to.

conclude: to form a final judgment or decision; to reach as logically necessary by reasoning; to shut up or close.

convocation: a gathering together; a ceremonial assembly.

corrupt: to rot; alter from the correct form; to become morally debased; tainted.

covenant: a written agreement or promise usually under seal between two or more parties, especially for the performance of some action.

deceive: to cause to accept as true what is false; to give a false impression; to fail to fulfill.

determine: to set ones mind to do; to fix the character, form, or position of beforehand; to fix conclusively; to limit in extent or boundary.

disannul: to make ineffective; to declare legally void

or invalid; to reduce to nothing; to desolate.

disinherit: to deprive of rights or previously held special privileges; to deliberately prevent from inheriting.

doctrine: system of belief; something taught; a teaching.

effect: meaning; being operable; to bring about a operation, intent, or reason.

elect / election: chosen for marriage at some future time; chosen for office but not yet installed; chosen.

elements: the factors determining the outcome of a process; the simplest principles of a subject of study; an ingredient or component.

enmity: mutual ill-will, often concealed.

exalt: to elevate in position or power; to glorify; to give honor to

exclude: to cast out of a place or position previously occupied; to prevent the entrance of.

exhort: to incite; to strongly urge or provoke.

foundation: a body or base upon which something is built up; a basis (such as a principle) upon which something is supported.

glorify: to give honor or praise to; to elevate to the heavenly realm; to light up brilliantly.

gospel: the message concerning Christ, the kingdom of God, and salvation; an interpretation of such message; one of the first four New Testament books.

grace: undeserved divine assistance for human salvation; unmerited favor or mercy.

grieve: to burden; to cause distress or sorrow.

justify: to prove or show to be just or right; to qualify oneself by taking oath to the ownership of a property; to treat as righteous or worthy of salvation.

labour: to give out mental or physical effort; to work, especially when difficult.

leaven: a substance or element (such as baking powder) used to produce a controlled break down of an energy-rich compound (such as dough); something that lightens; a cause to be raised.

legalism: strict, literal, or excessive conformity to a moral code; the restriction of free choice.

manifest: to infest; to make known; understand or recognize by the mind; perceive by the senses, especially by sight; a public display of power or purpose.

Messiah: the expected deliverer of the Jews.

ordinance: something ordained or decreed by fate or a deity; a law or natural occurrence set forth by a governmental authority.

perdition: state of wickedness or sin; loss; eternal damnation or utter desolation; hell; an element in it's highest possible oxidation state.

pervert: to twist the meaning or sense of; to cause to turn away from what is true or morally right; to divert to a wrong purpose; to corrupt; a person given to twisted desire, especially sexual.

predestinate: to destine or determine before; to foreordain to an eternal destiny or fate by divine decree.

principle: a doctrine; the laws of nature underlying

the working of something; a code of conduct.

provocation / provoke: to arouse to a feeling or action; to incite to anger.

purge: the removal of elements or members regarded as undesirable or disloyal; to cast out.

purpose: a plan; a reason (for doing something); a determination or goal; something set up as an end to be attained; an intention.

redeem: to free from what distresses or harms; to free from captivity by payment of ransom, to buy back.

repent: to turn from sin and dedicate oneself to the amendment of ones life; to change ones mind; to feel regret.

reveal / revelation: an act of showing or communicating divine truth; making known; an enlightening or astonishing disclosure.

rudiment: a beginning; something unformed or undeveloped; a basic principle.

temptation: to provoke to do something.

transgression: violation of a law.

vain: without effect; having no value, worthless; having or showing undue pride.

Contact Darrell Gilbert
furnitureworks7@msn.com

Or order more copies of this book at

TATE PUBLISHING, LLC

127 East Trade Center Terrace
Mustang, OK 73064

(888) 361 - 9473

Tate Publishing, LLC

www.tatepublishing.com